KEEP ON TURNING ▶▶▶

AntiStress Mandala Coloring Book

KEEP ON TURNING

AntiStress Mandala
Coloring Book

YOUR FEEDBACK MATTERS!

Do you have any particular coloring book cravings, any themes or designs you'd just really like to see? Drop me a line and share them. Maybe I could make your coloring dreams come true!

This Coloring Book
Belongs to

_____

_____

_____

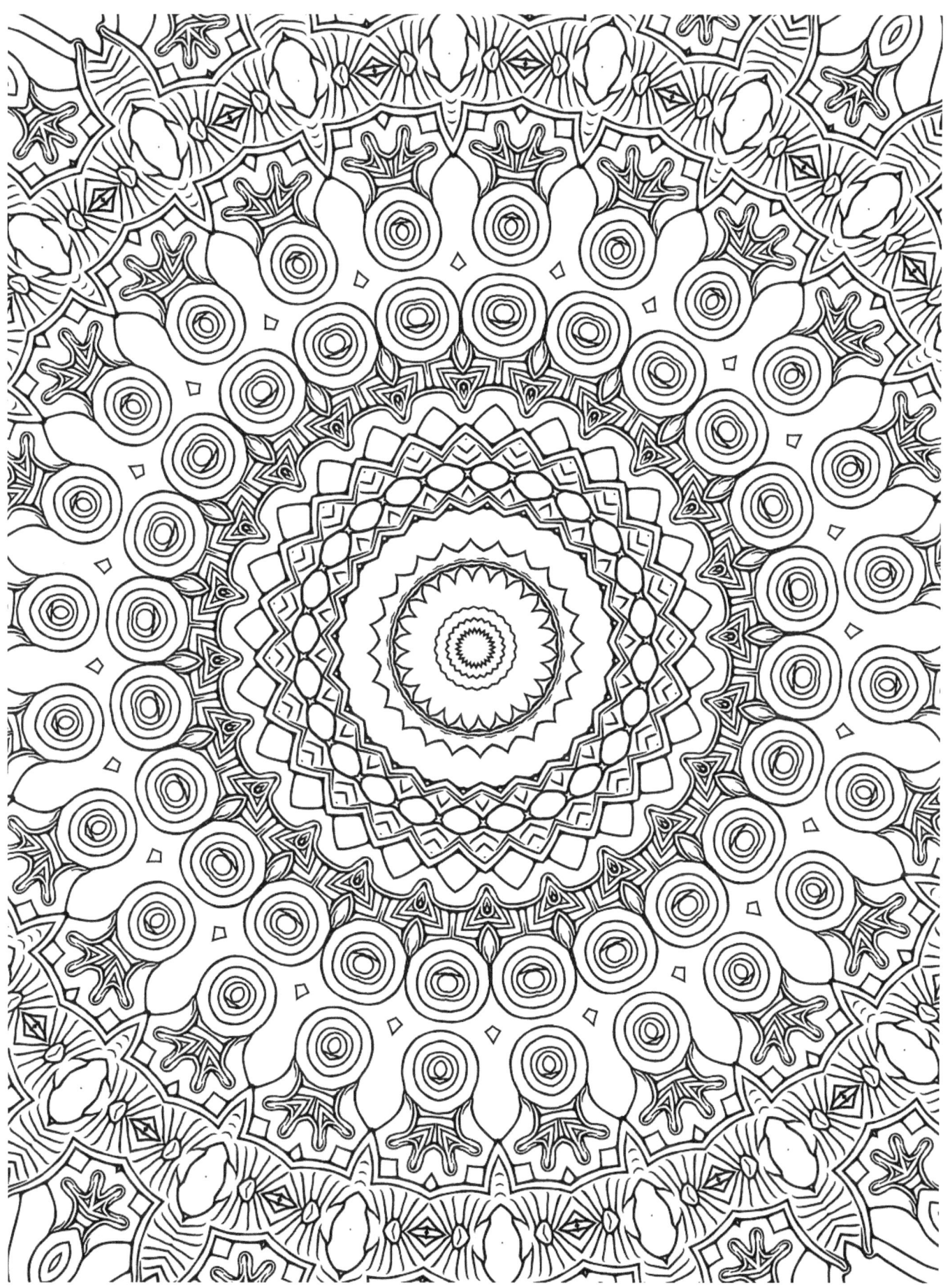

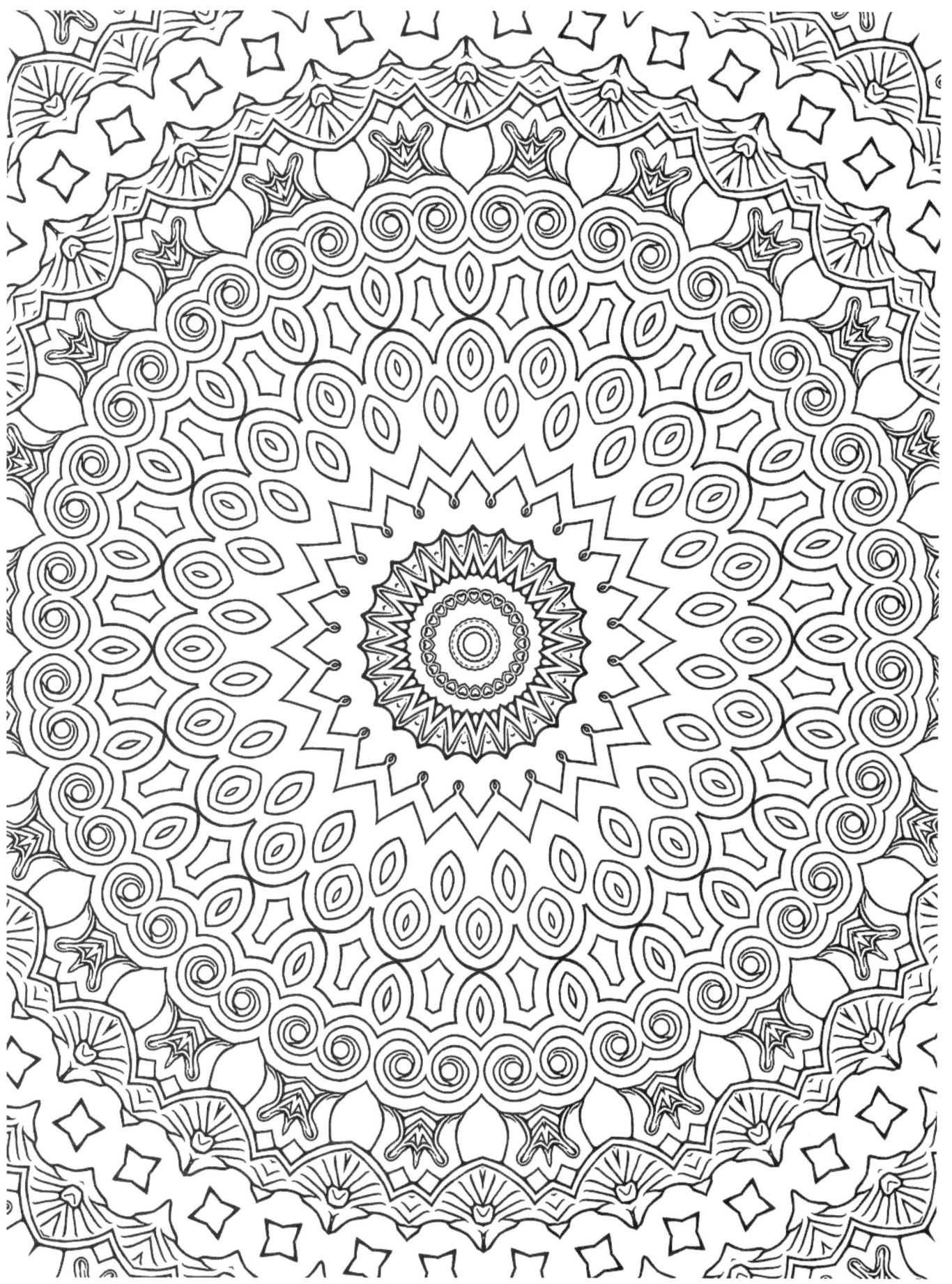

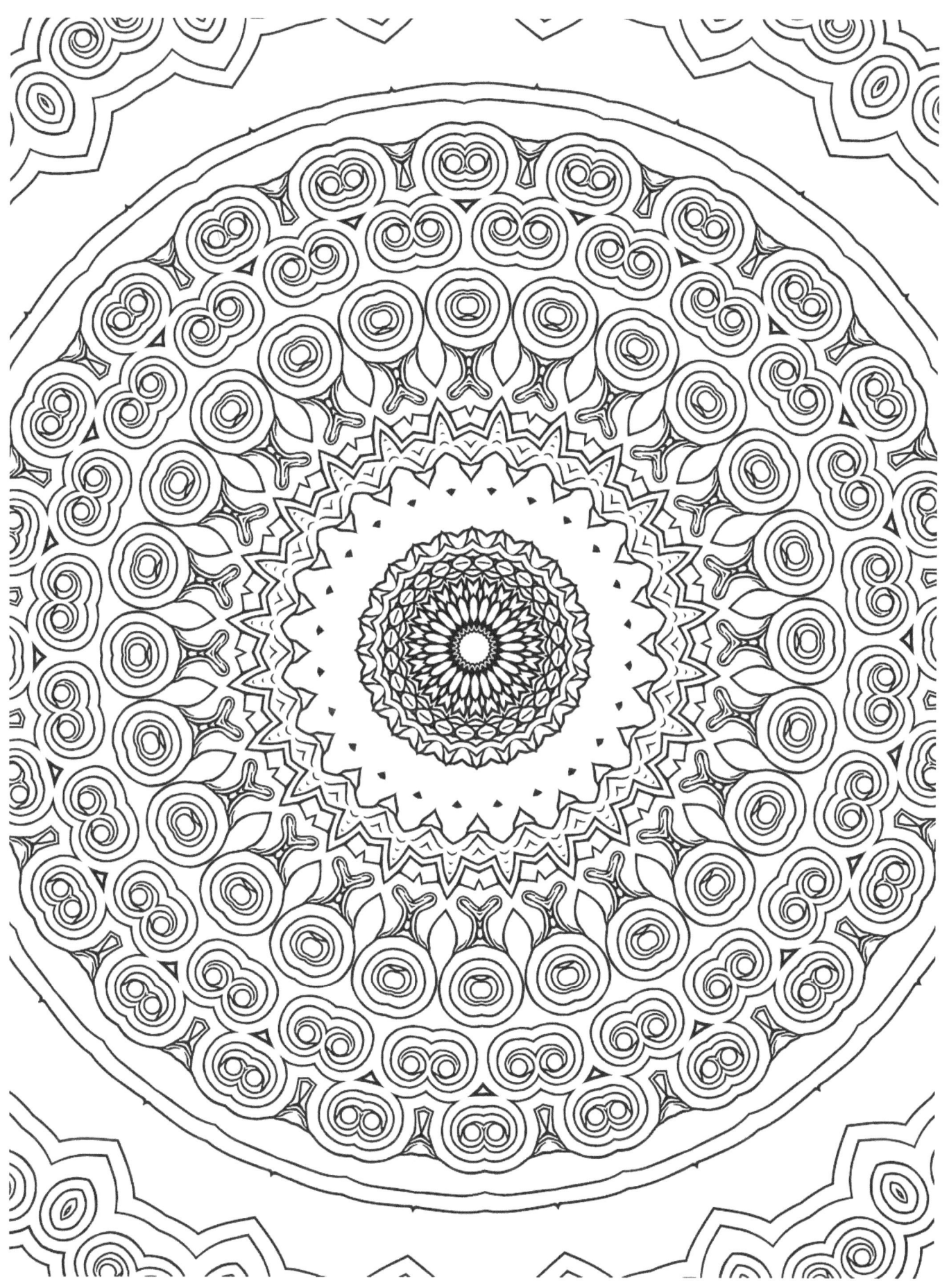

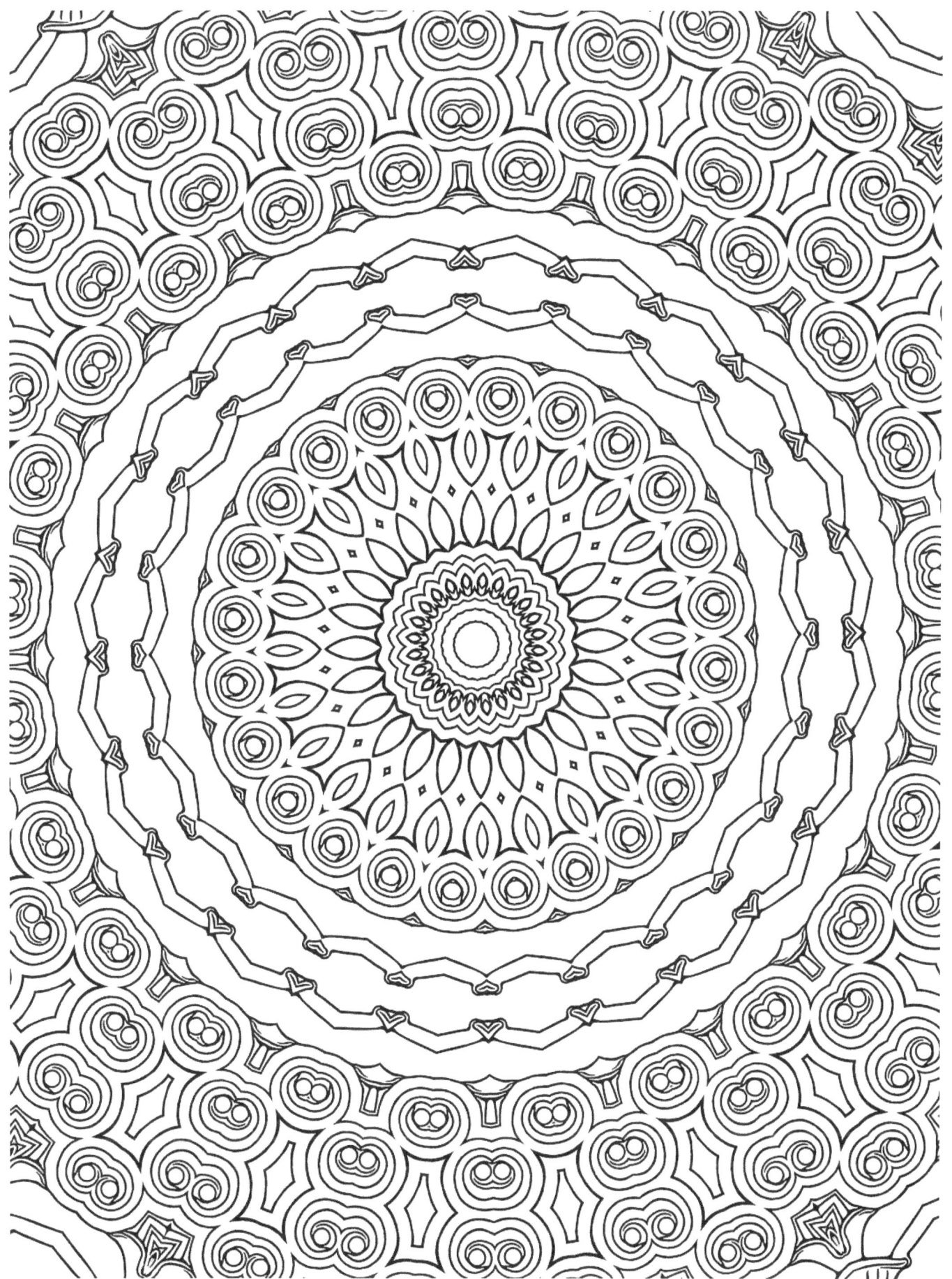

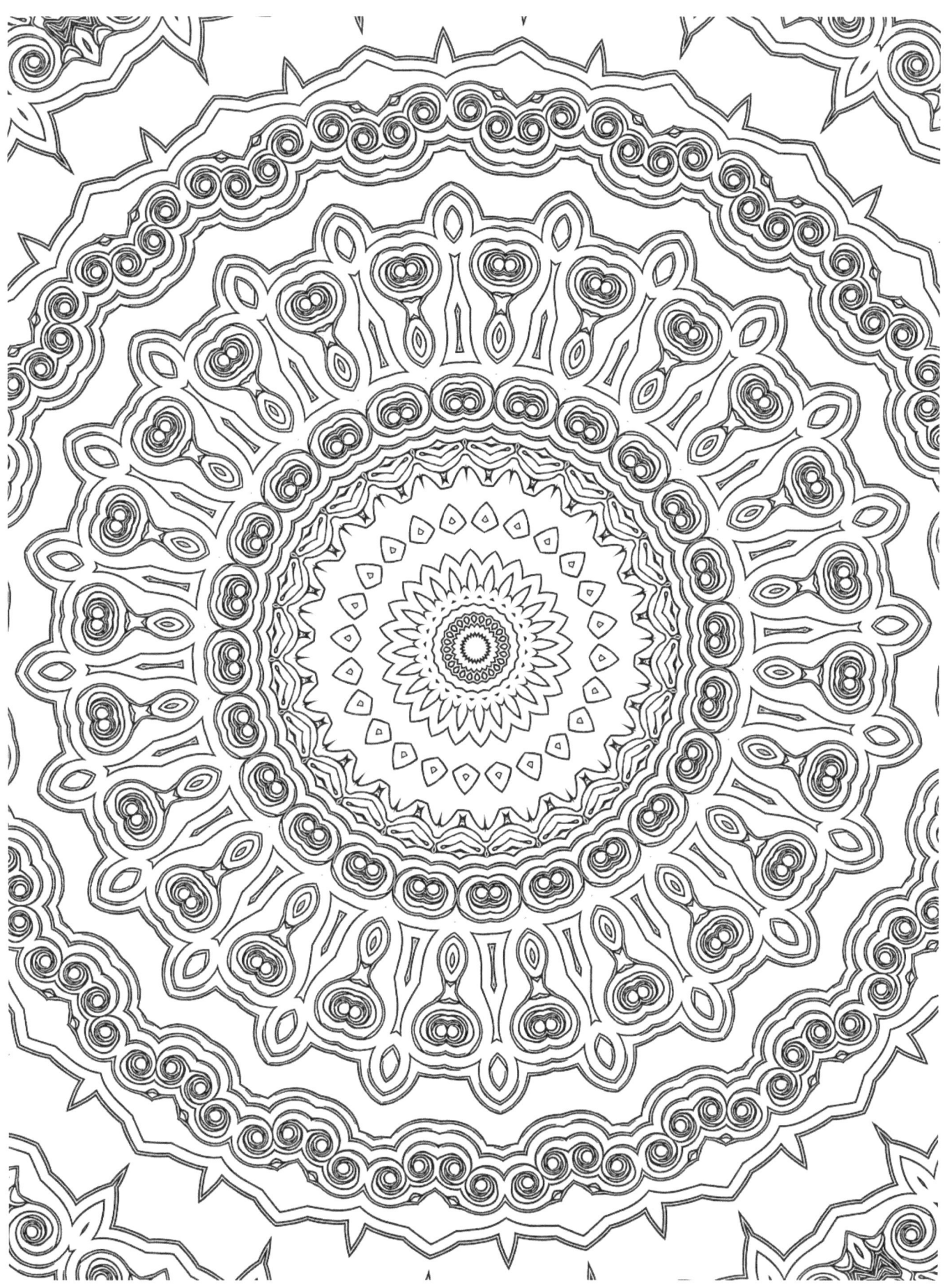

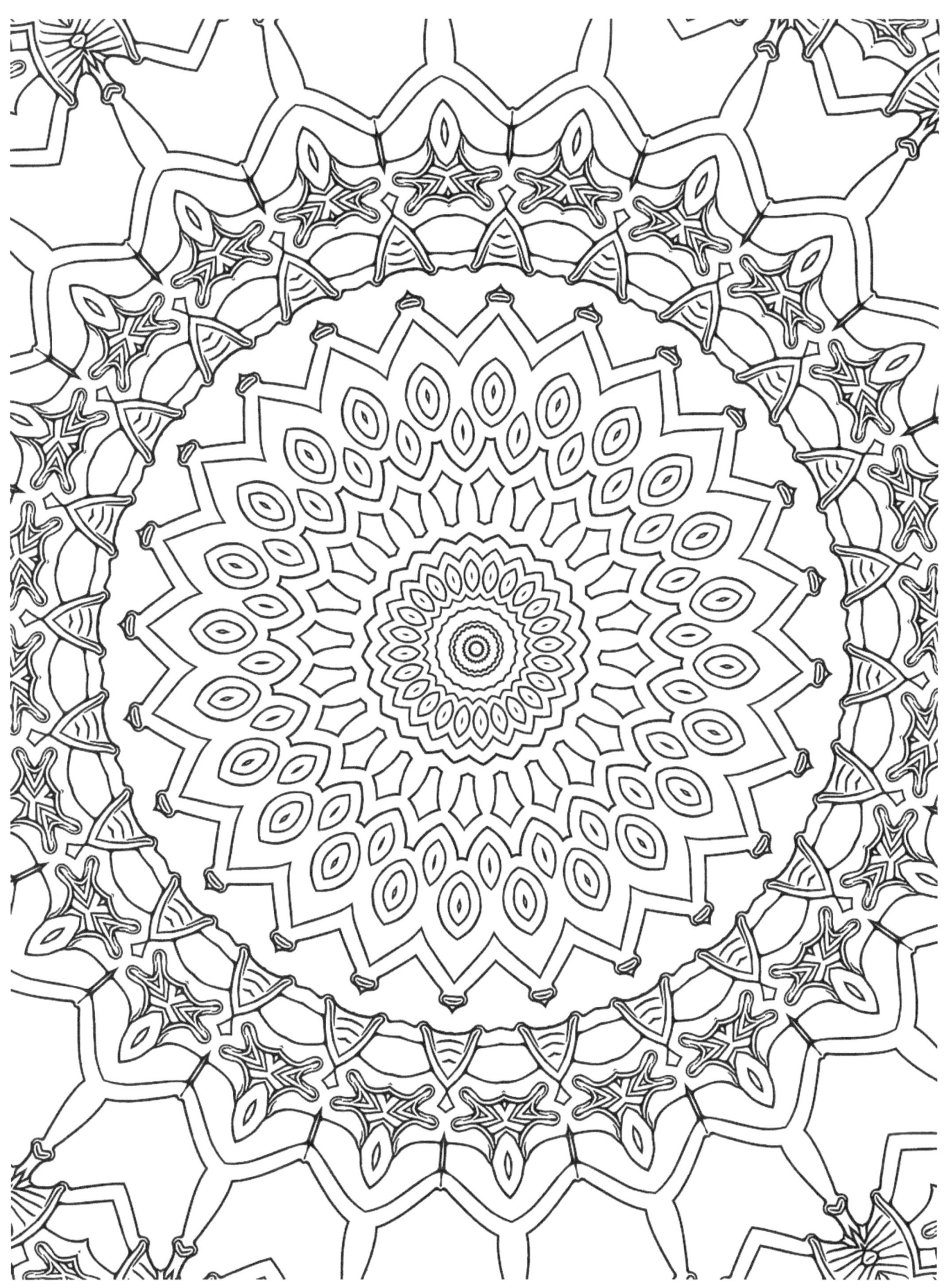

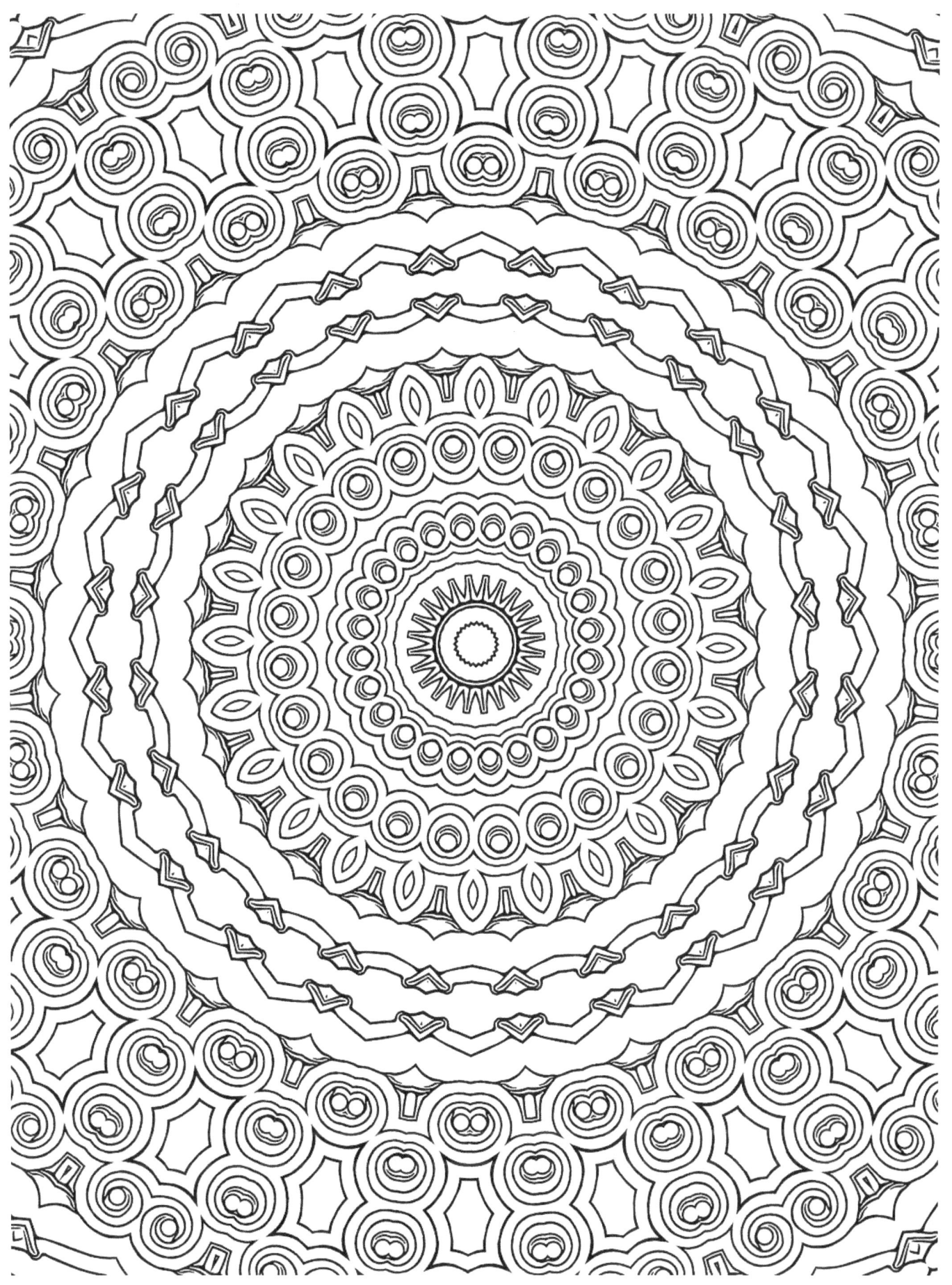

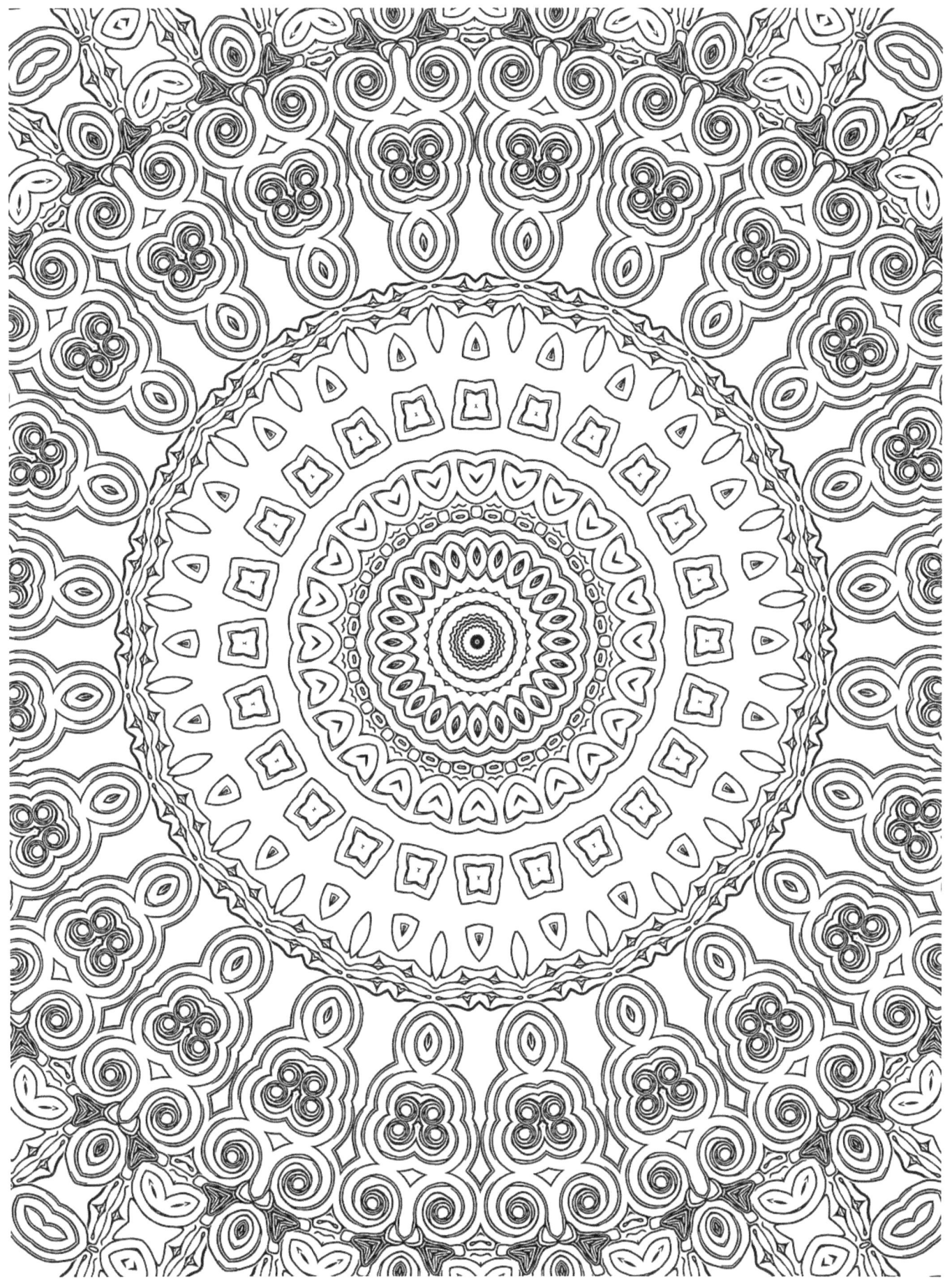

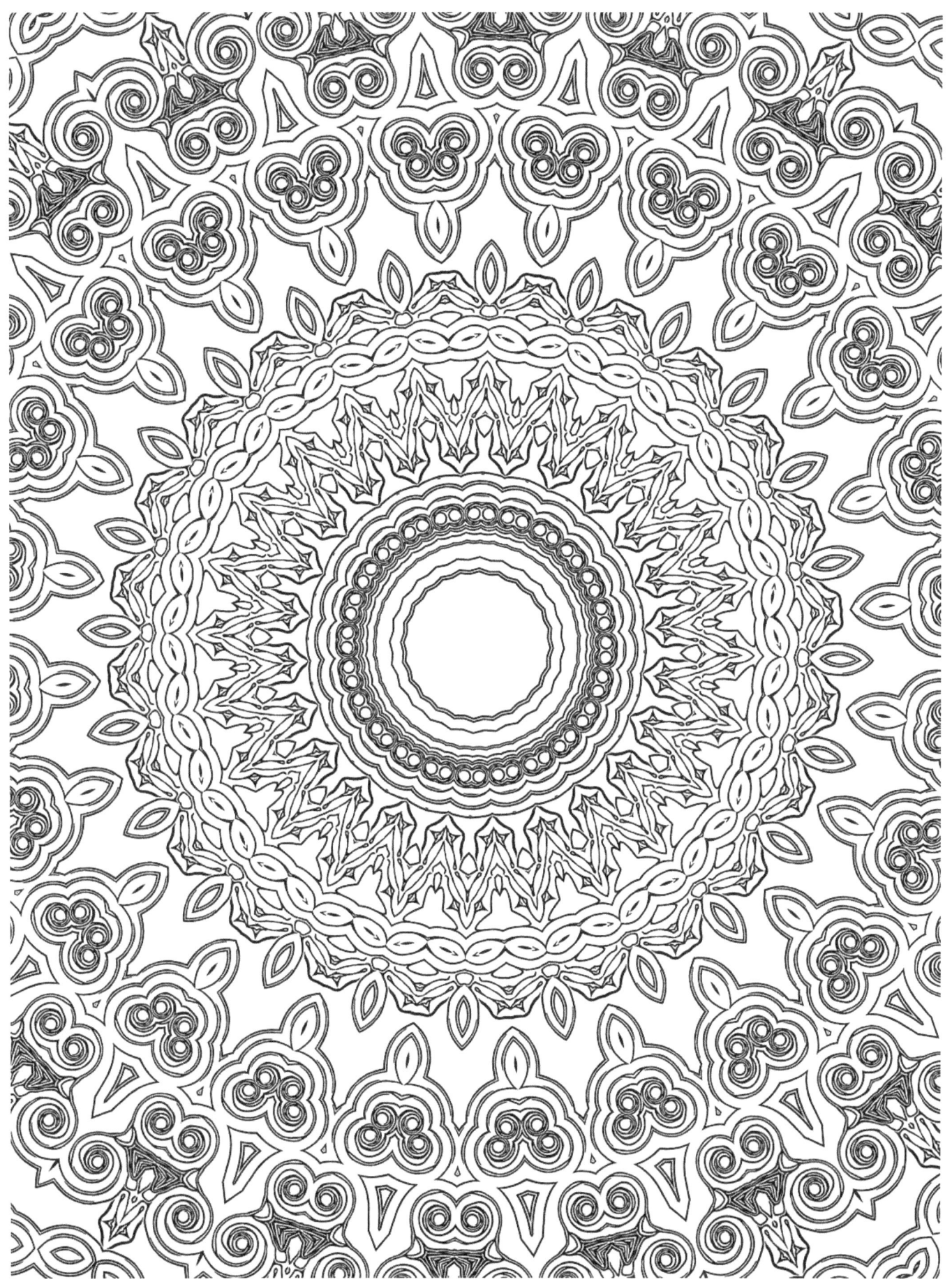

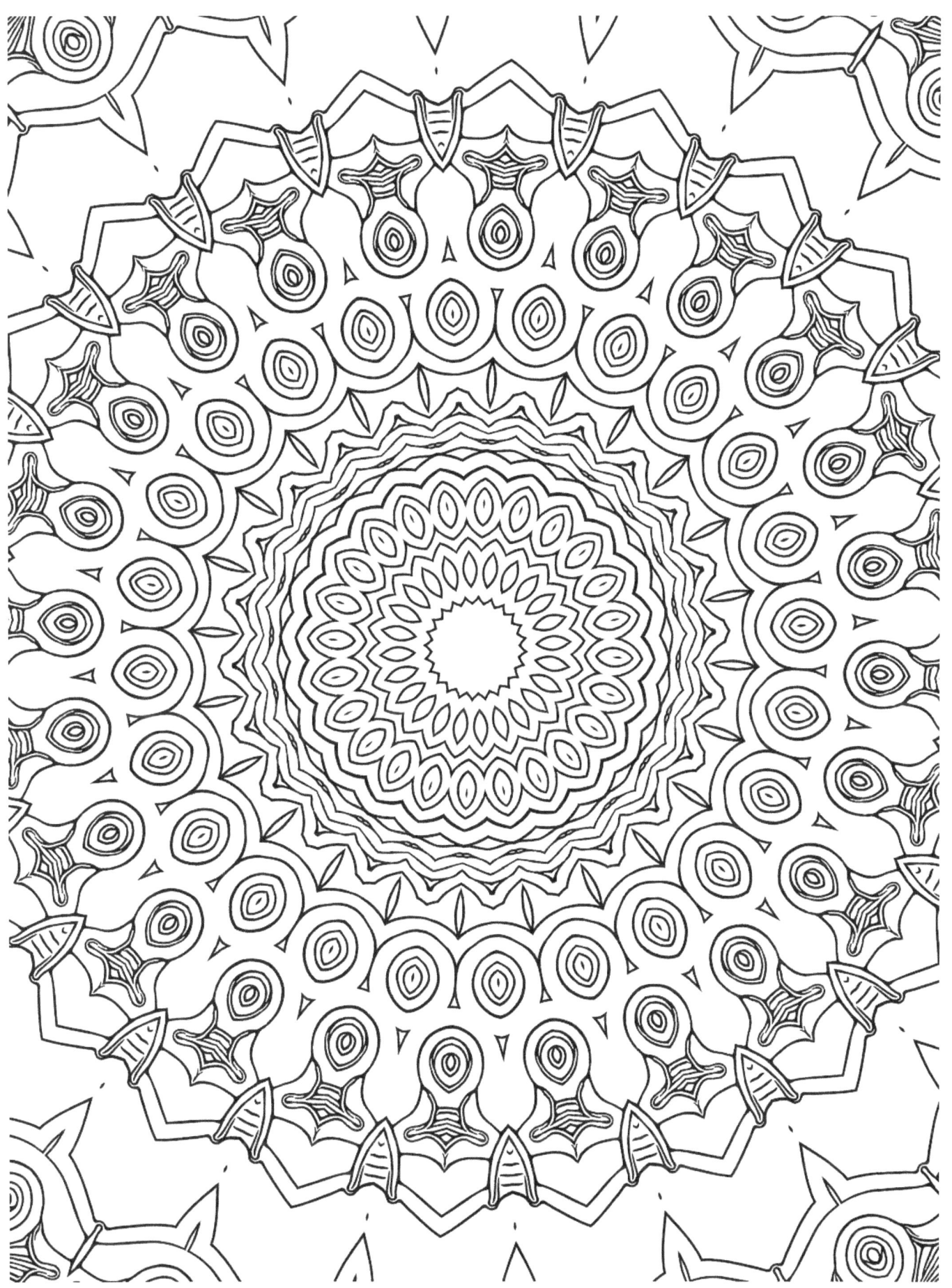

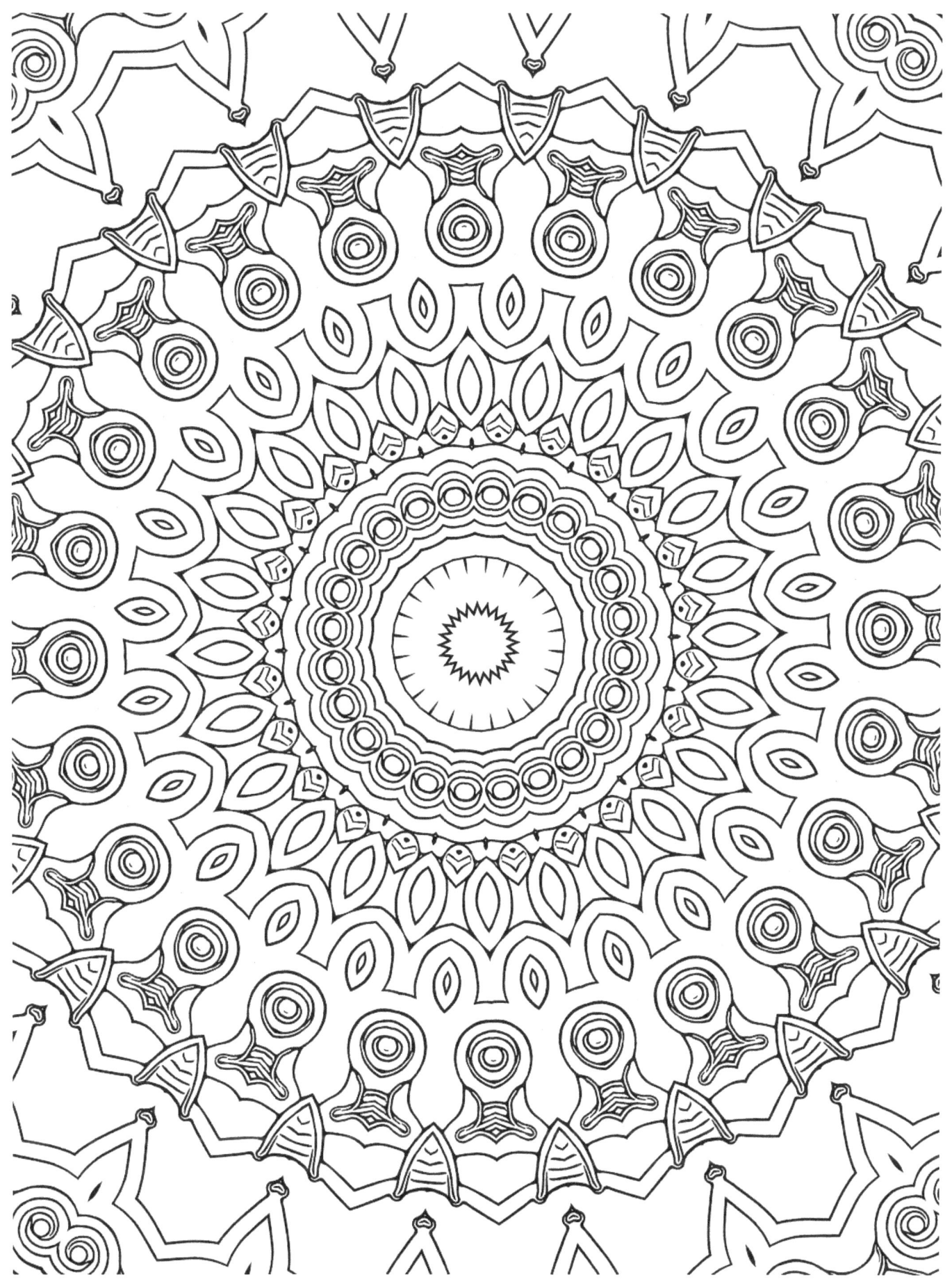

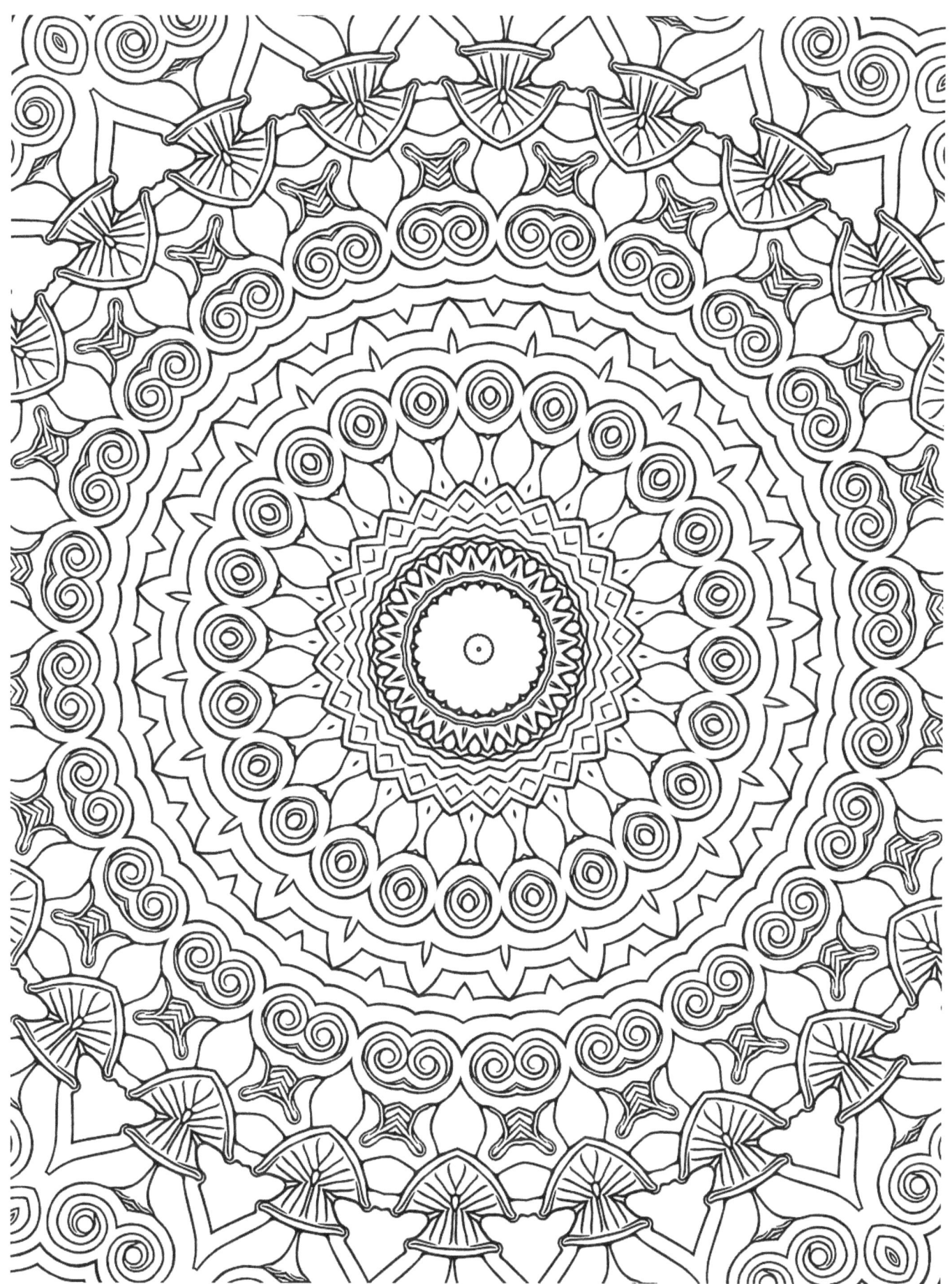

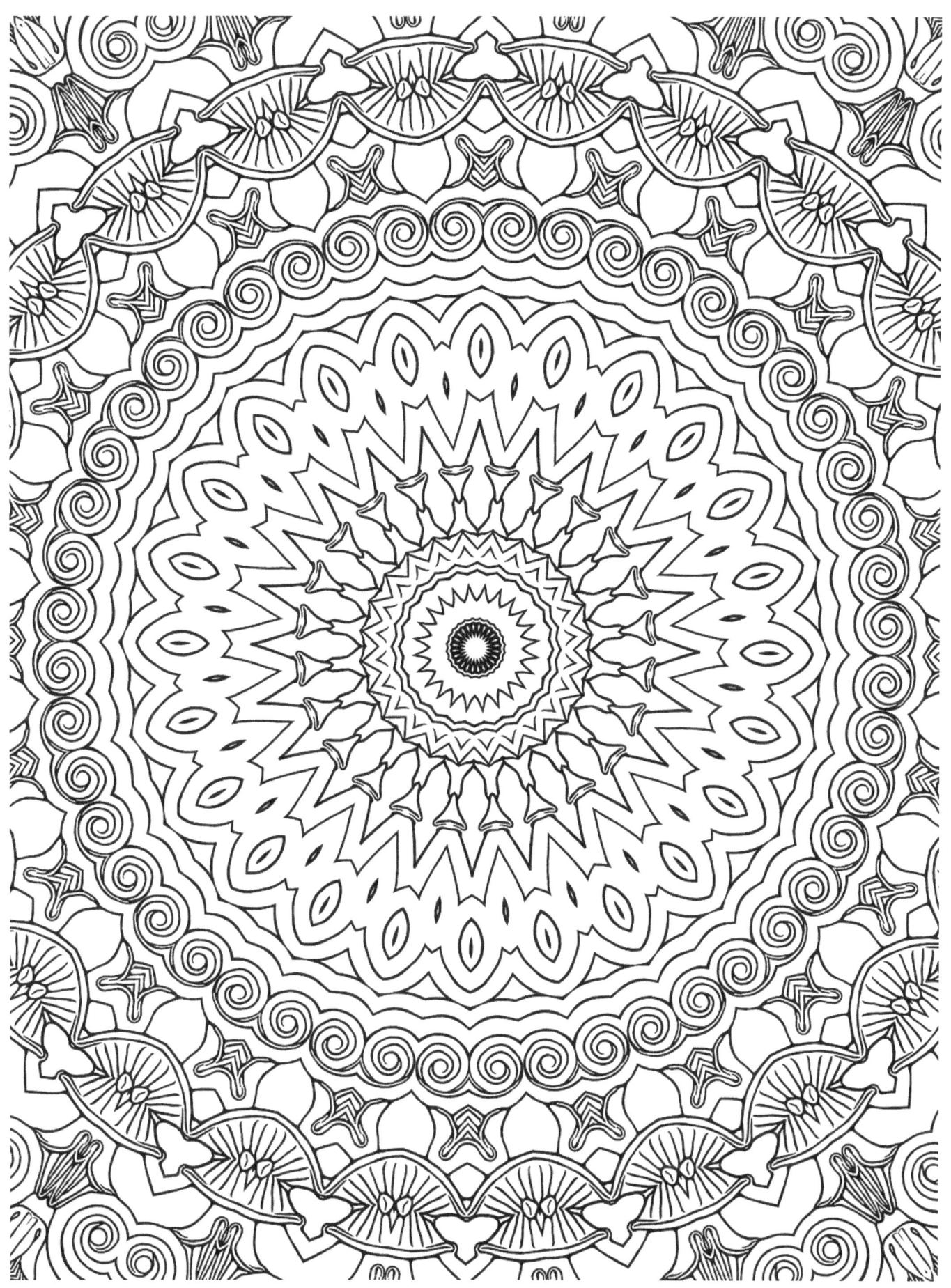

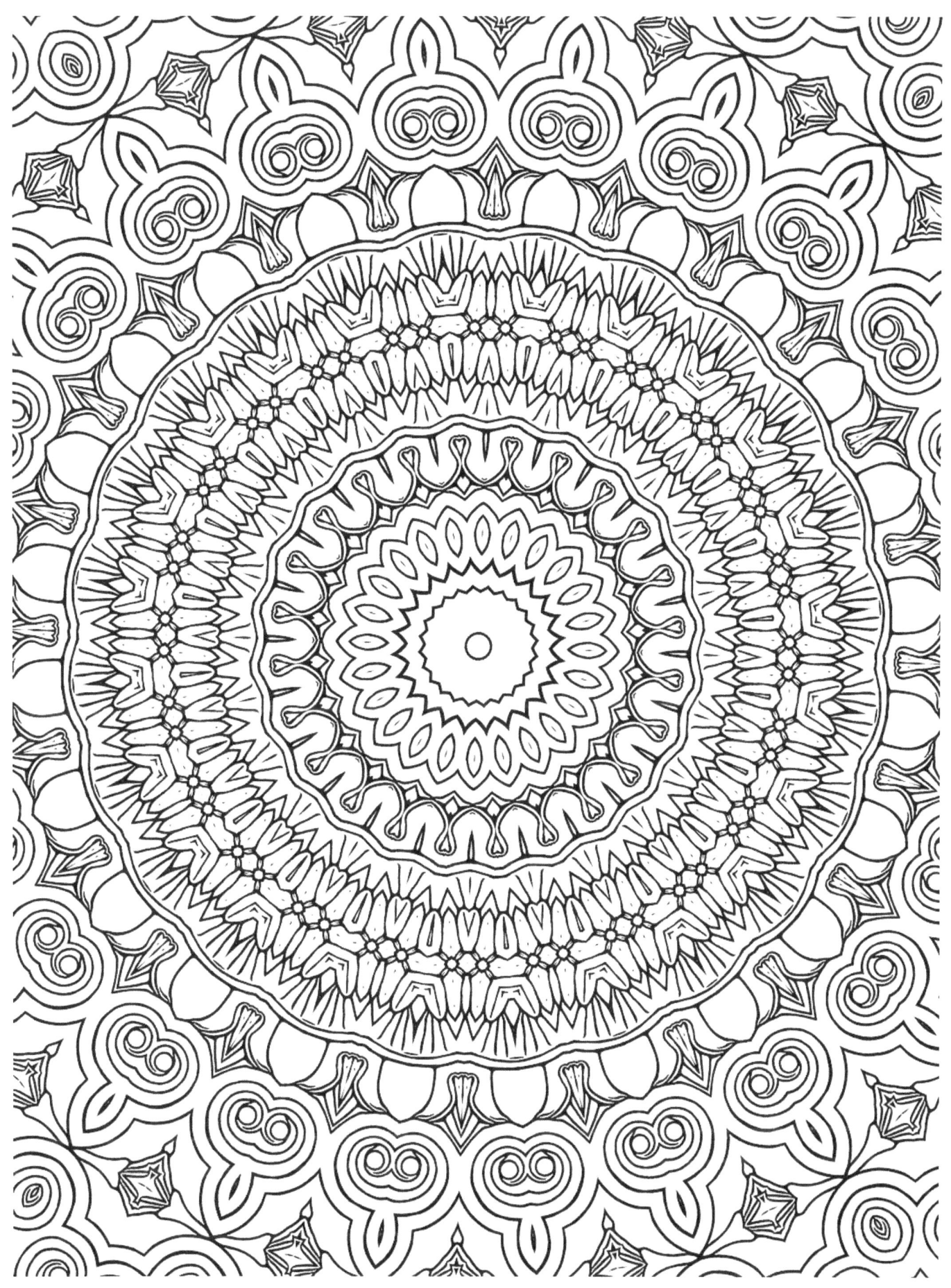

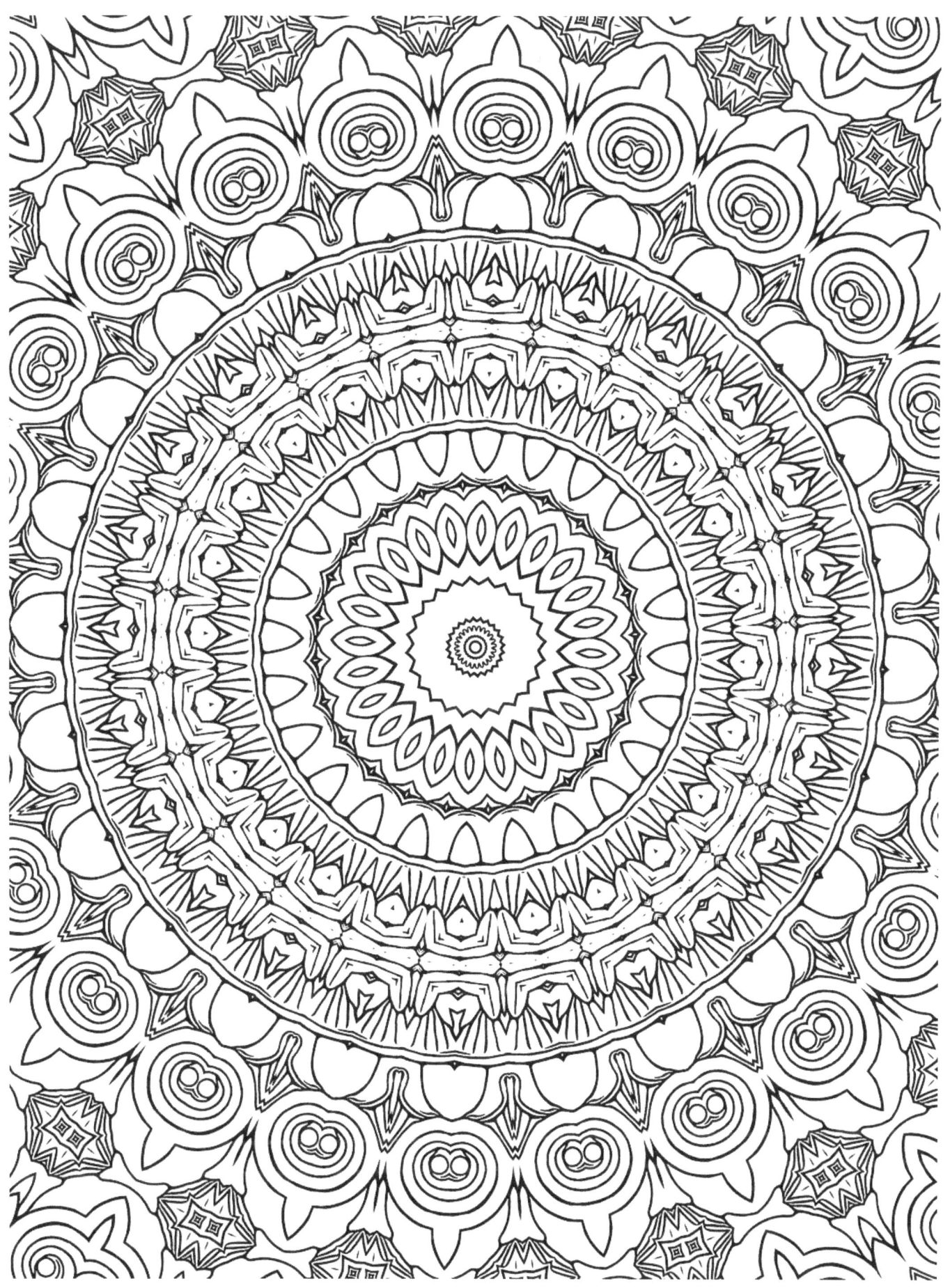

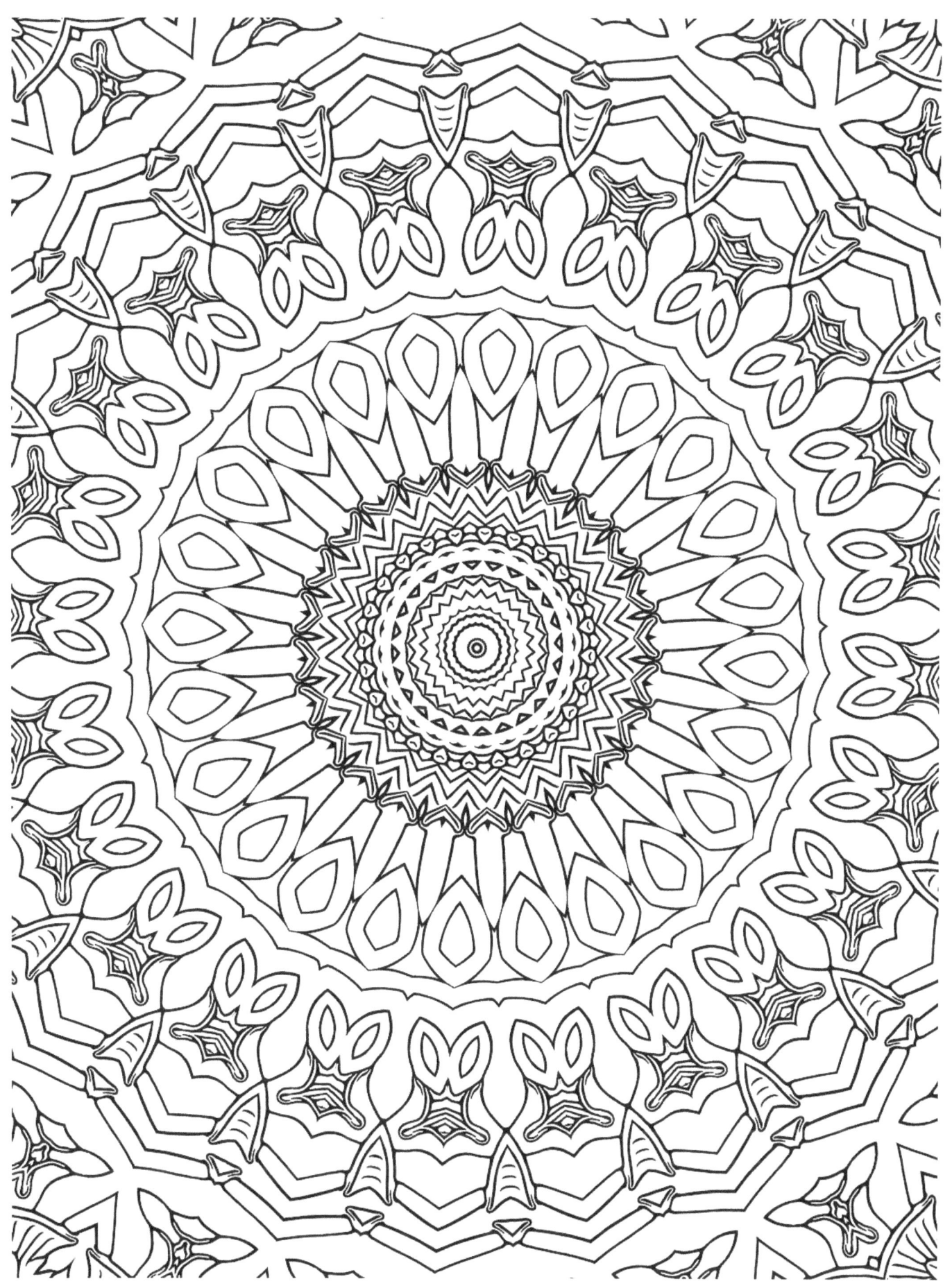

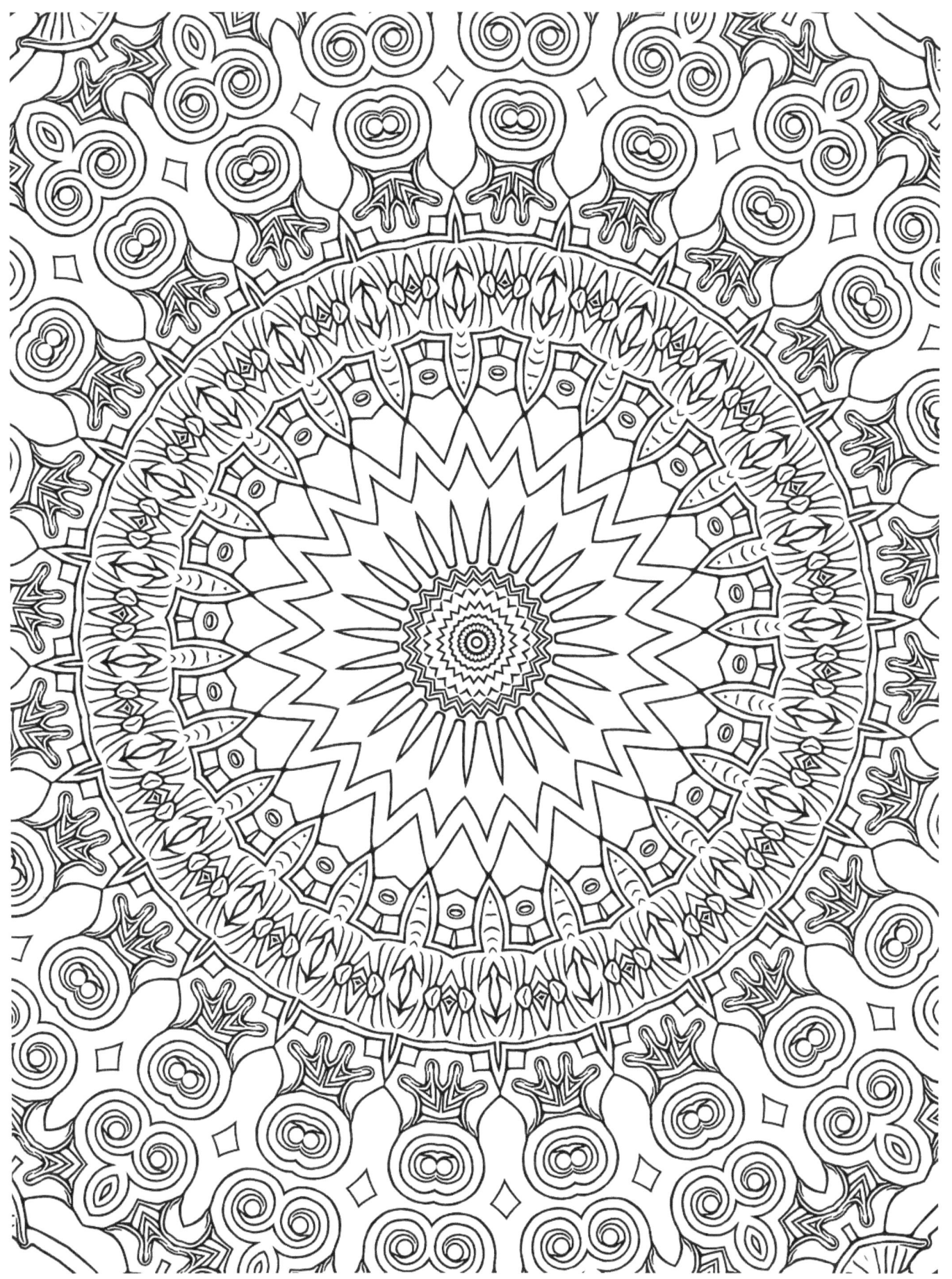

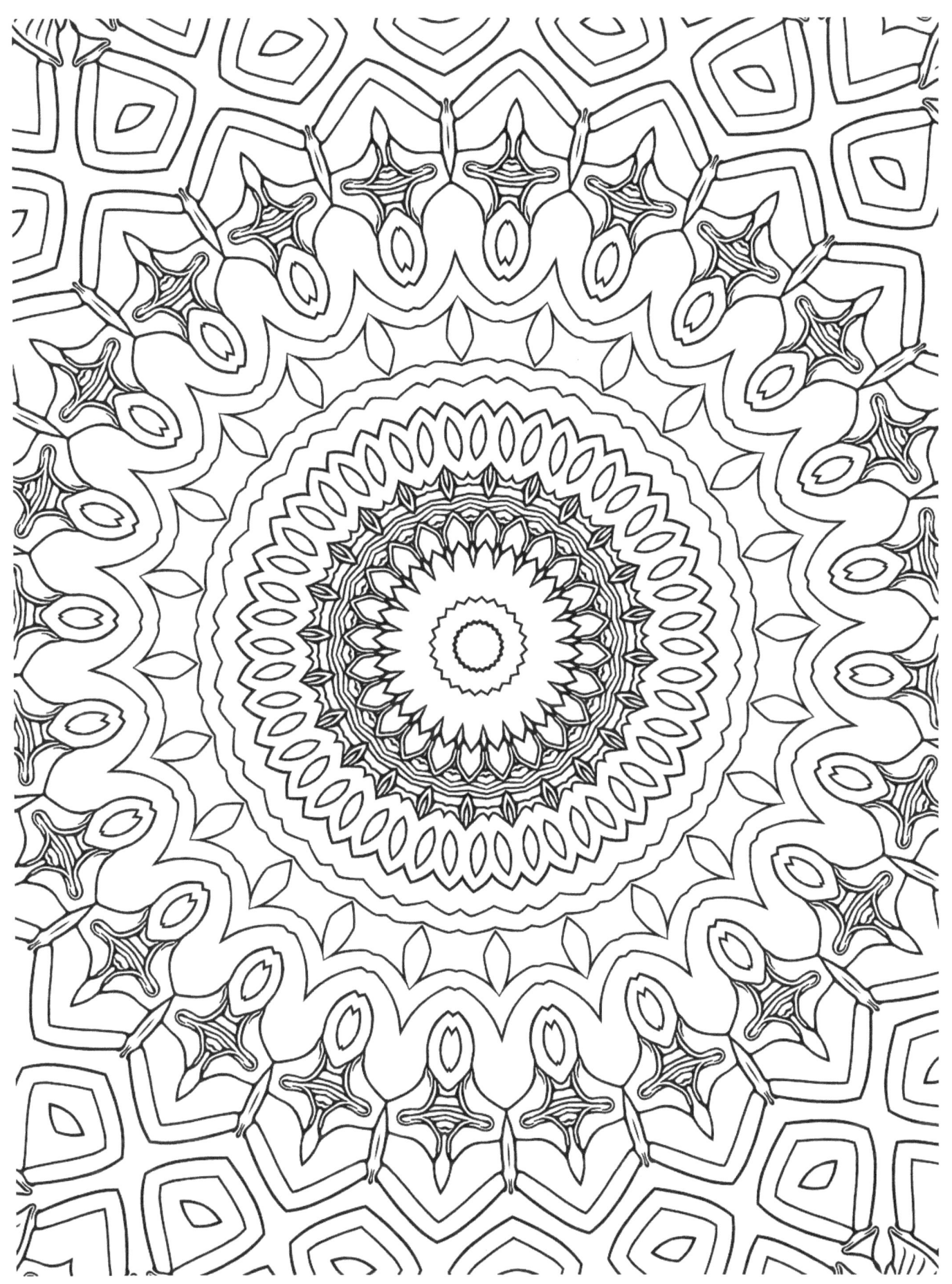

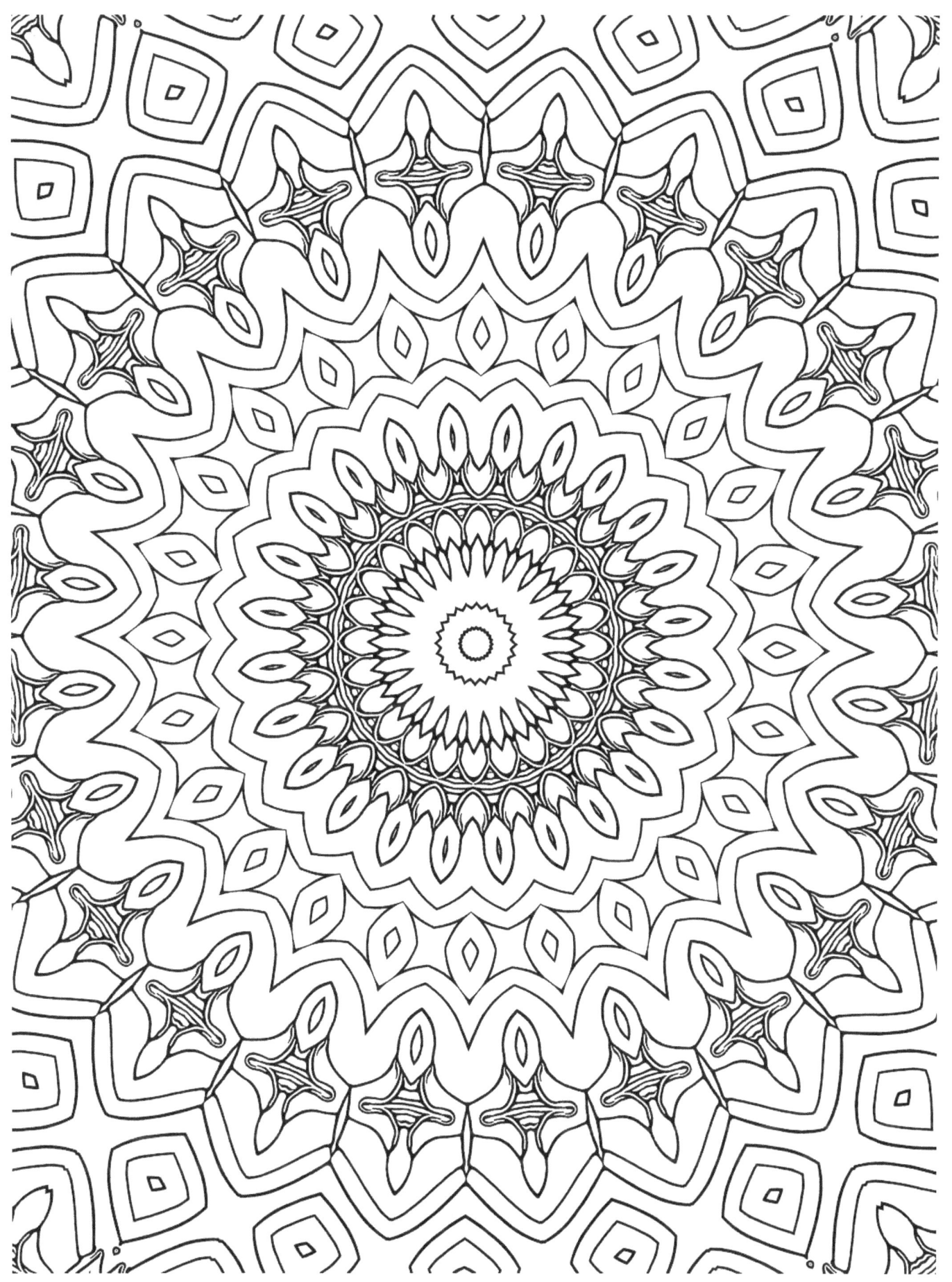

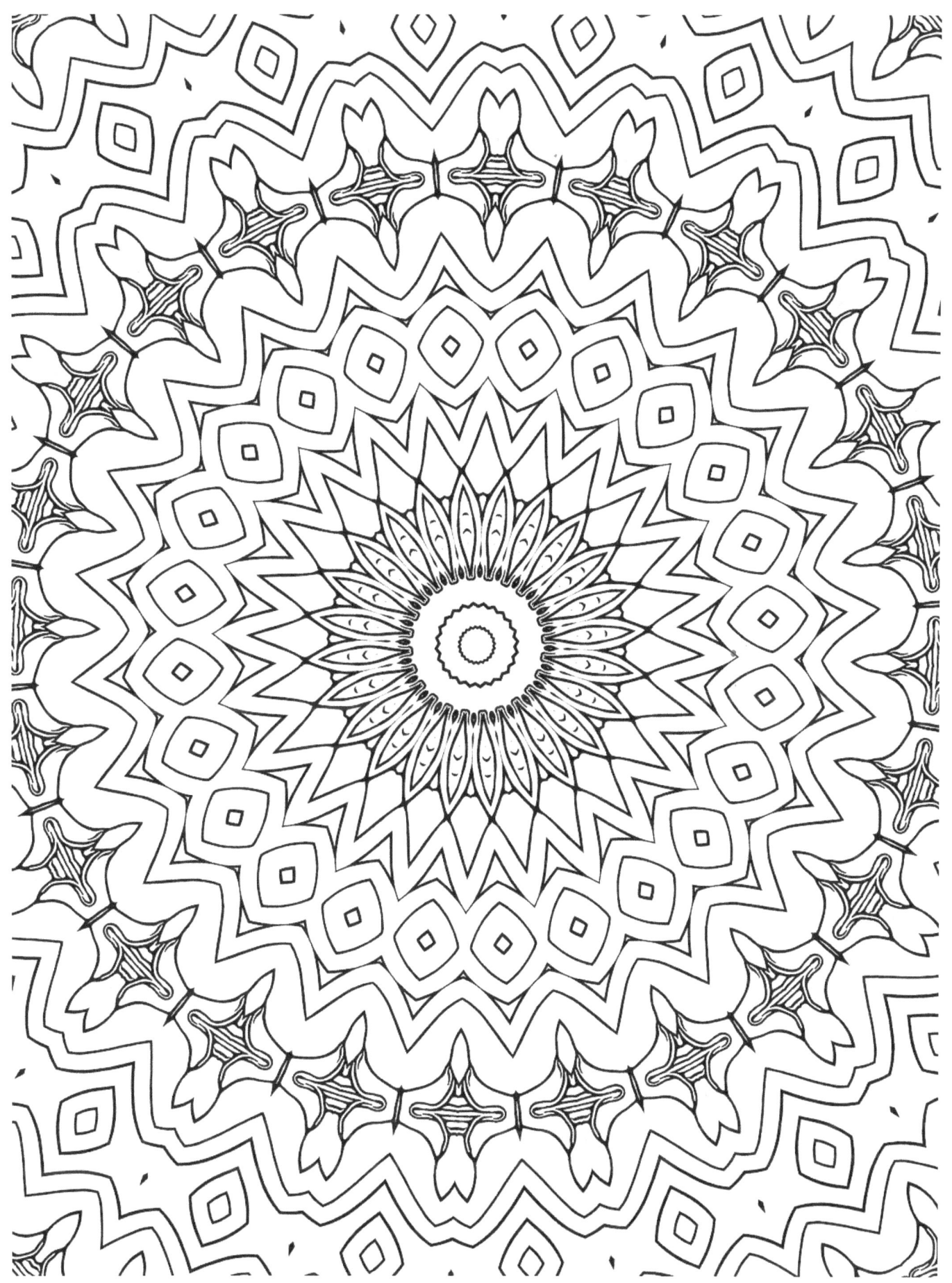

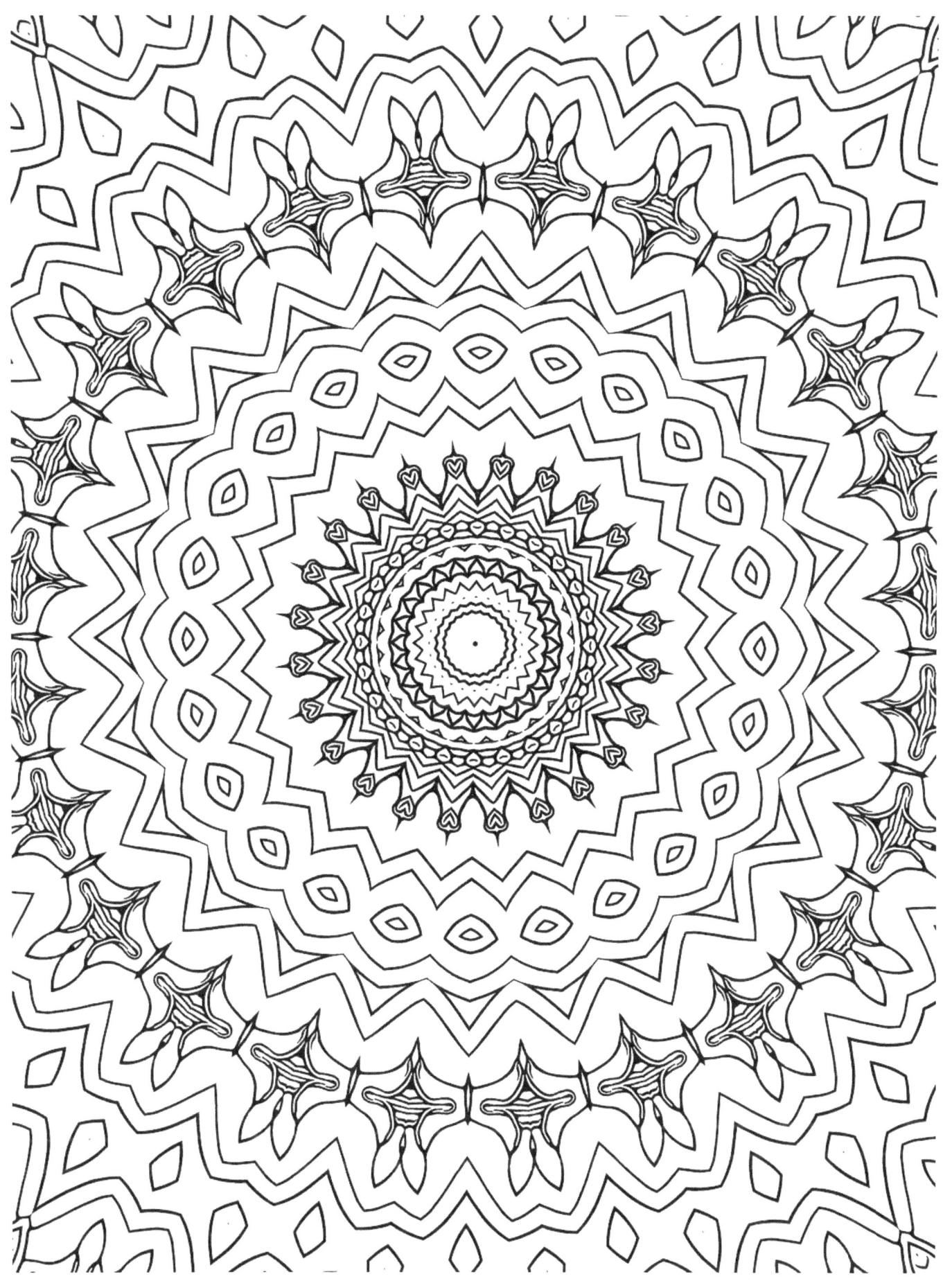

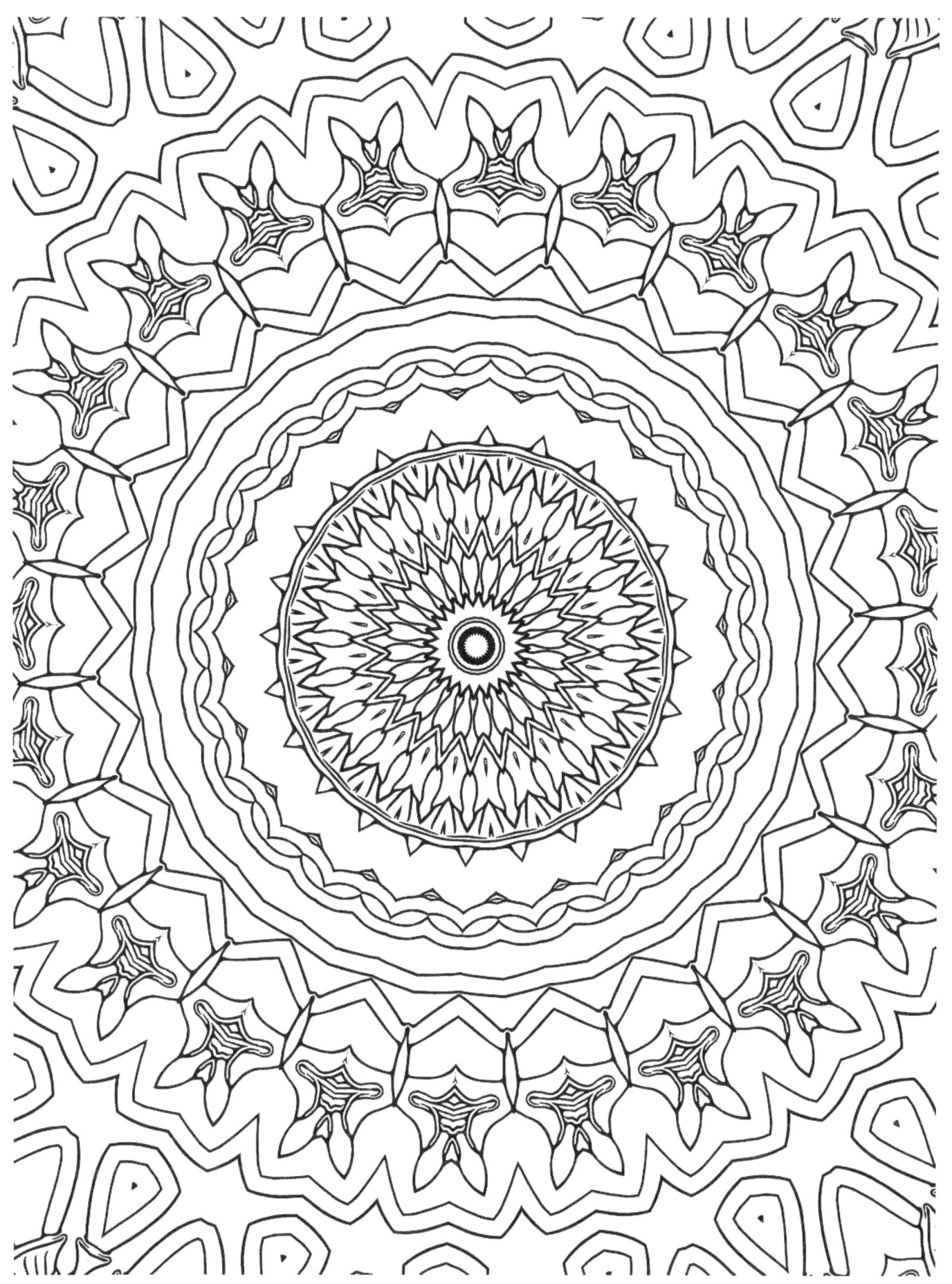

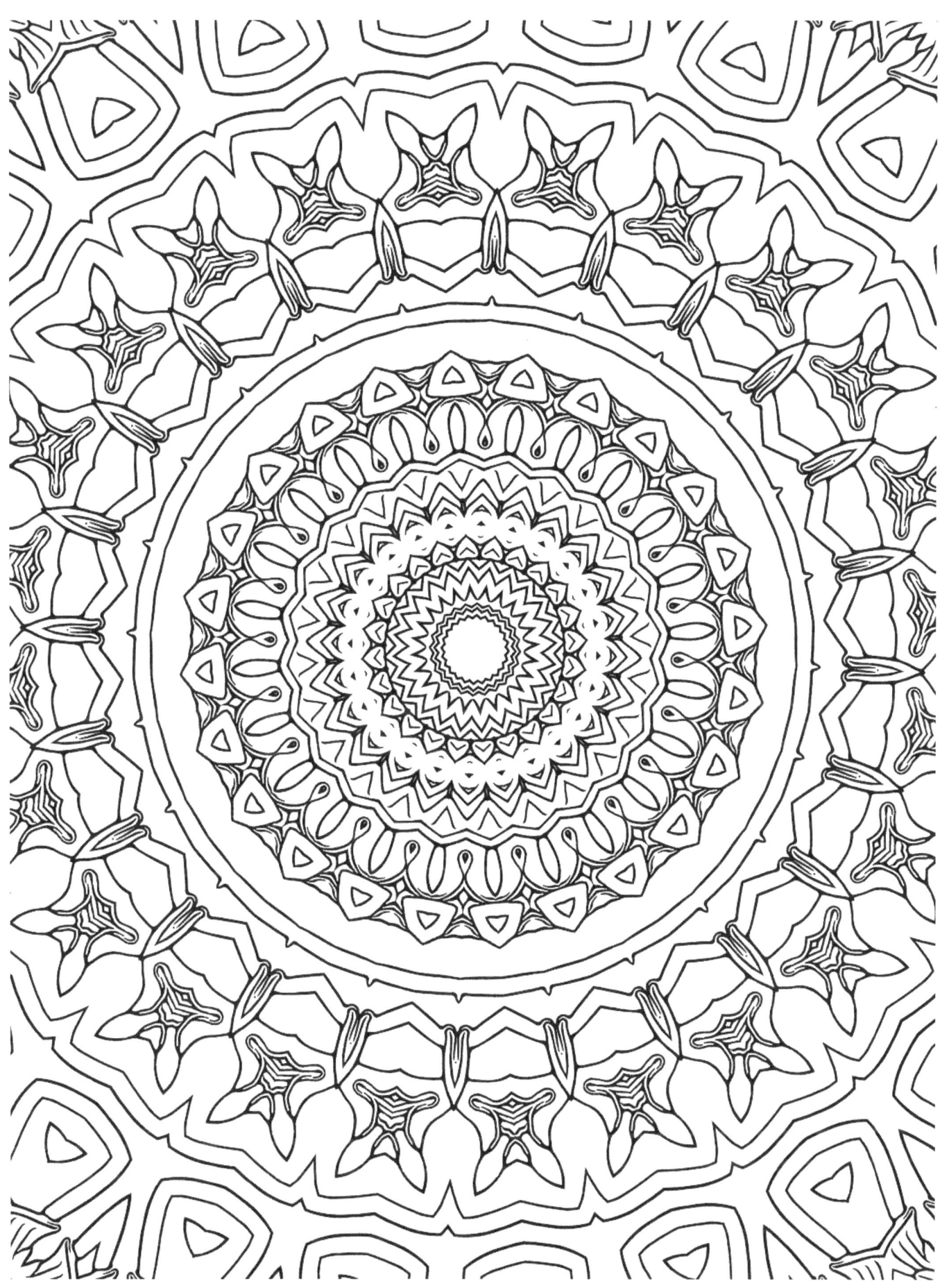

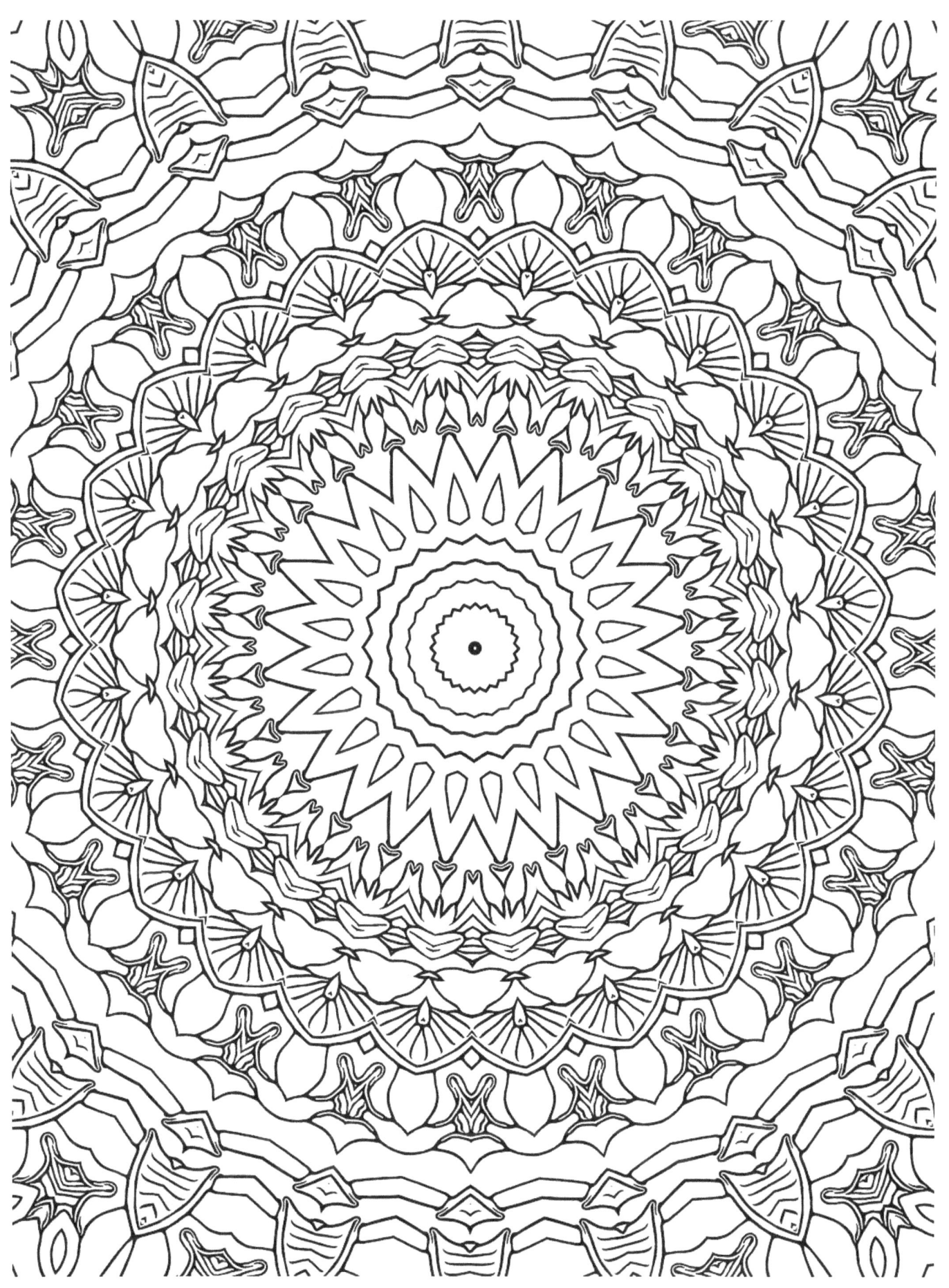

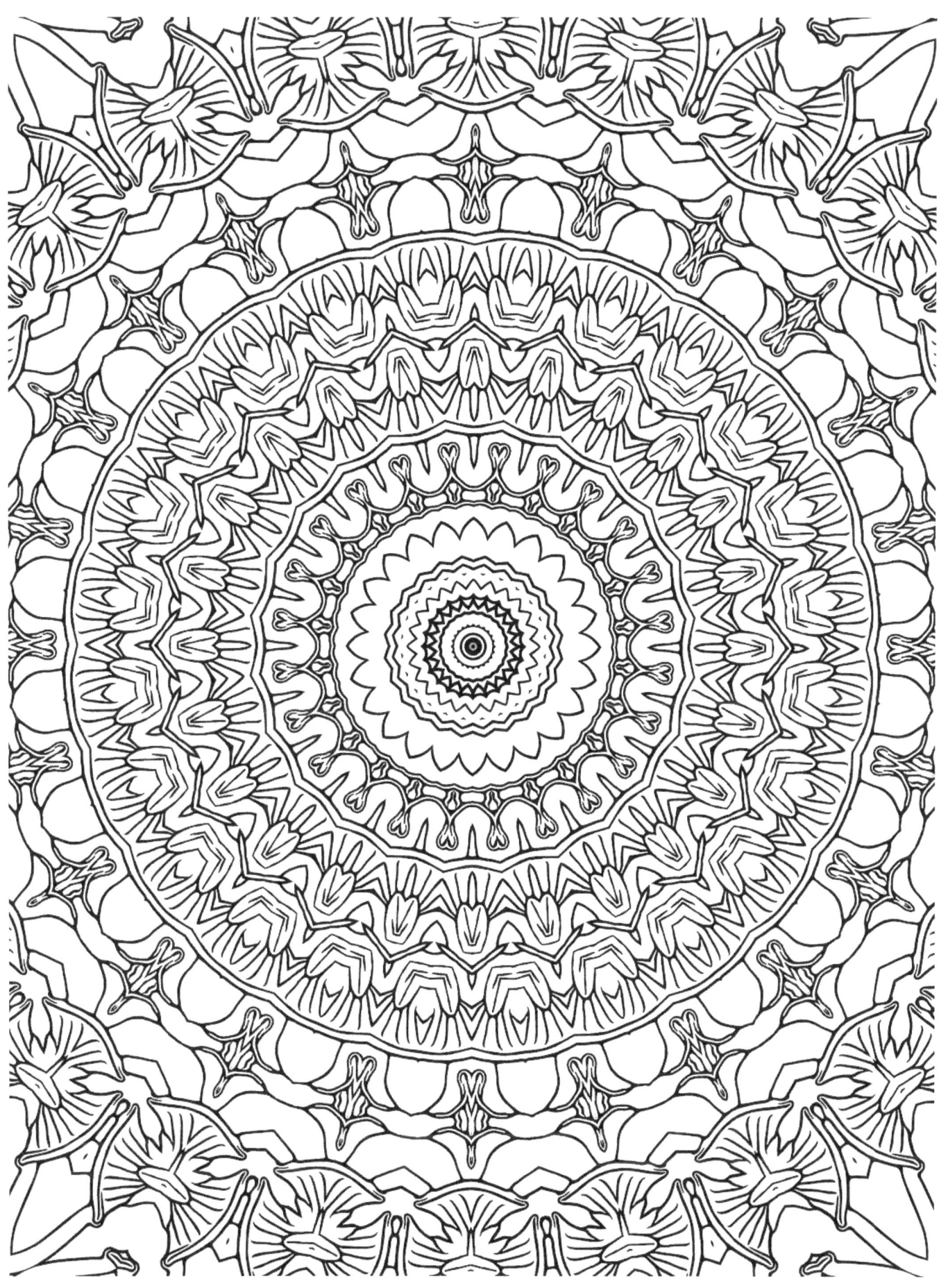

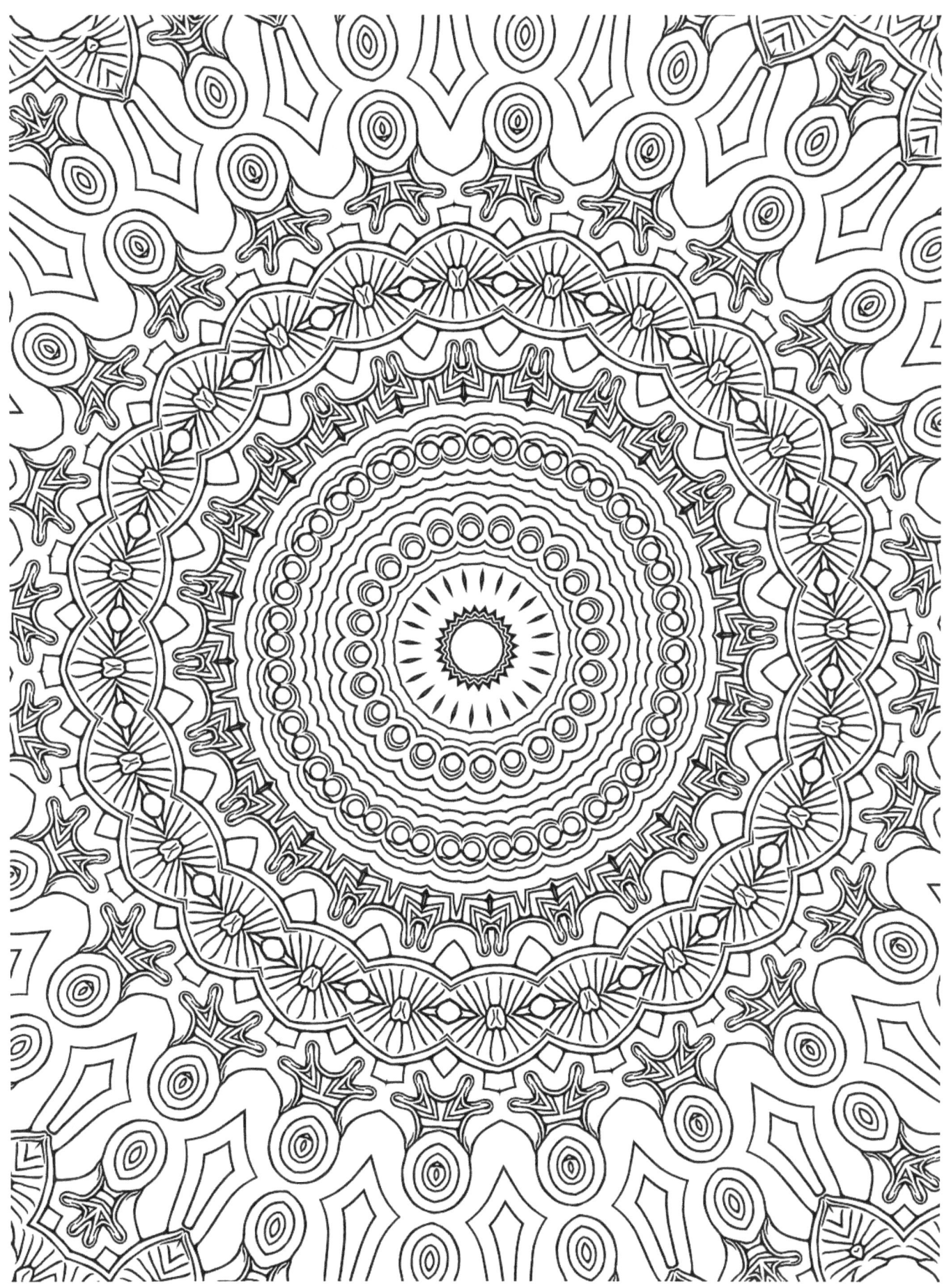

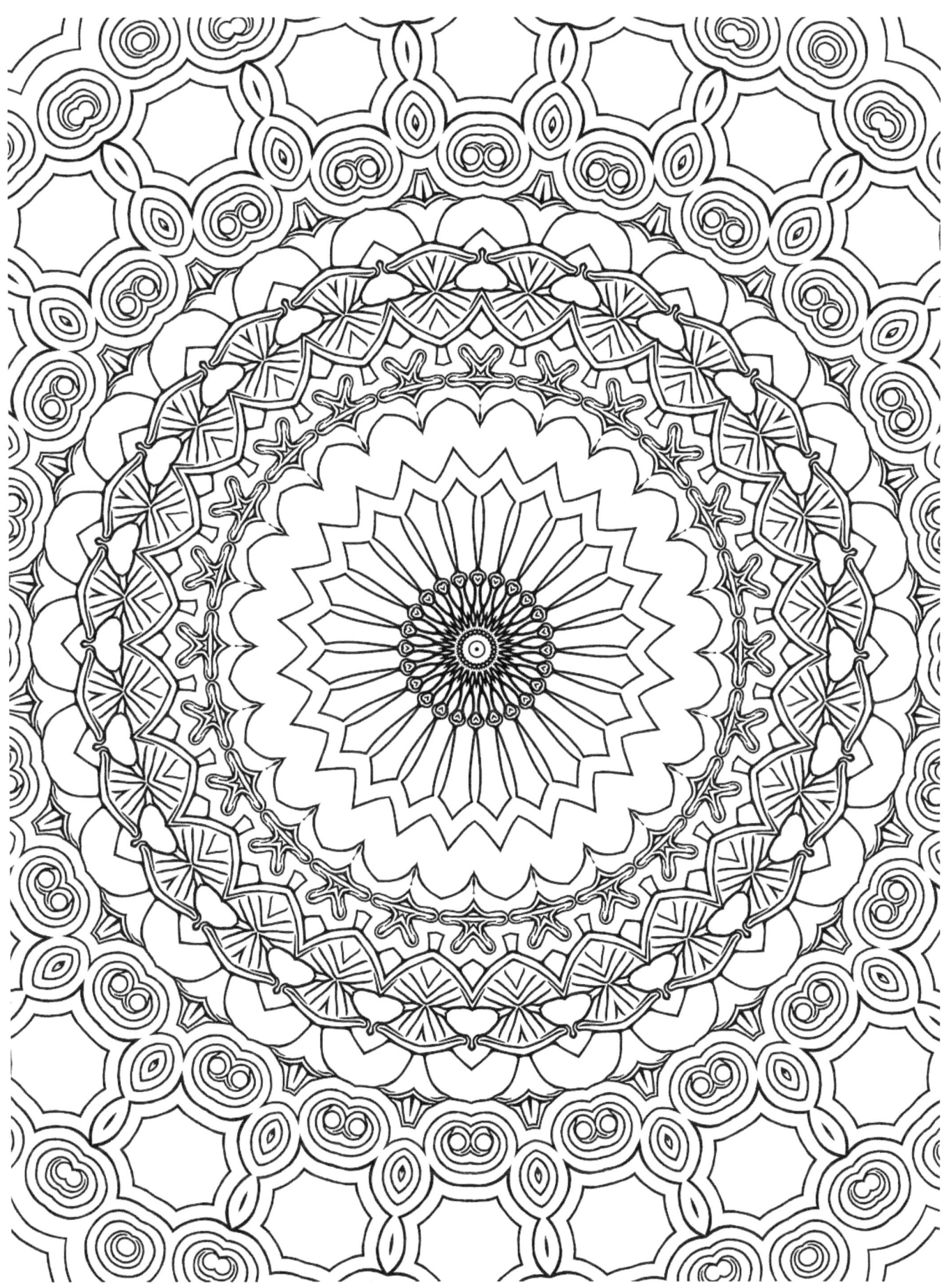

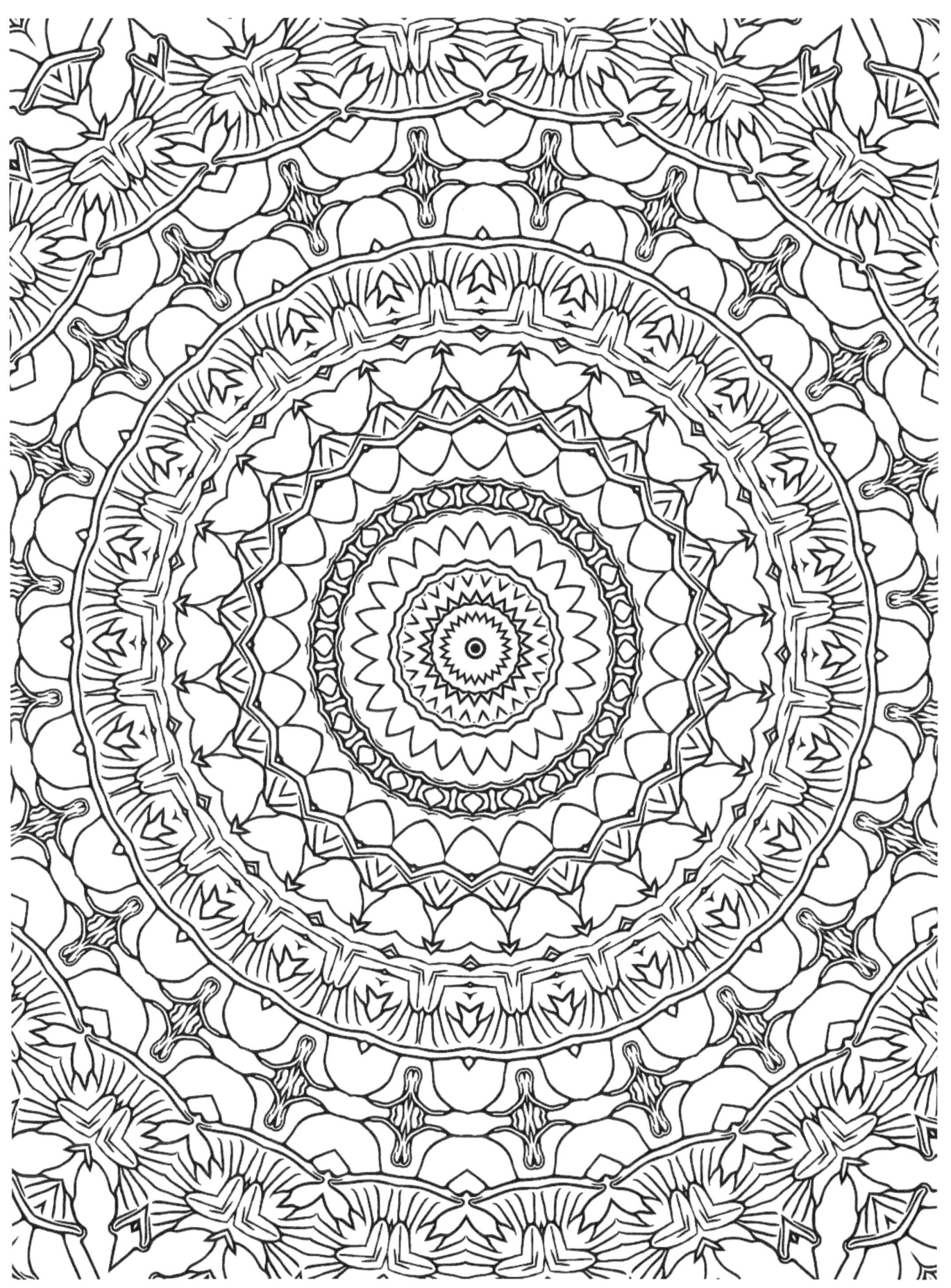

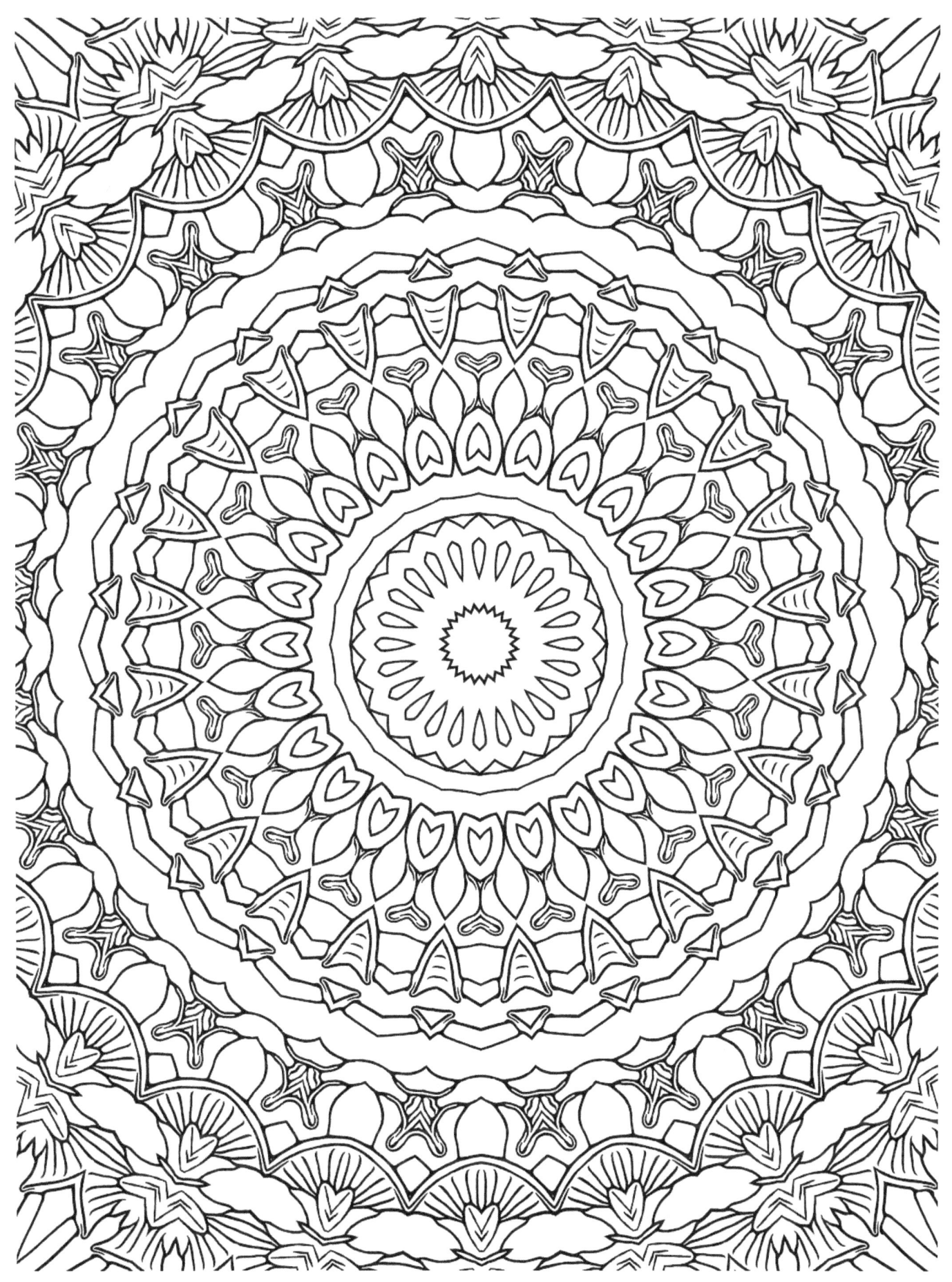

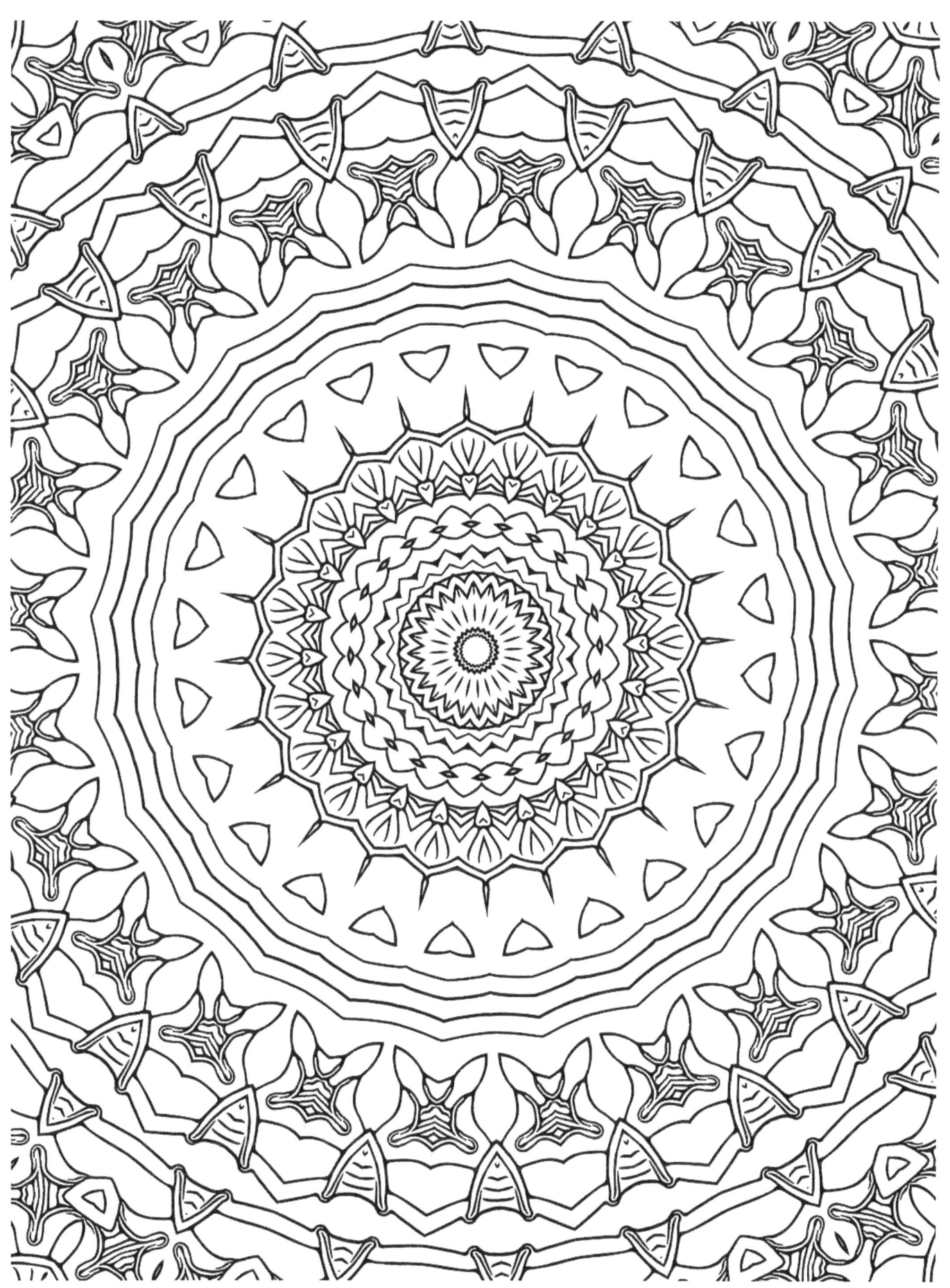

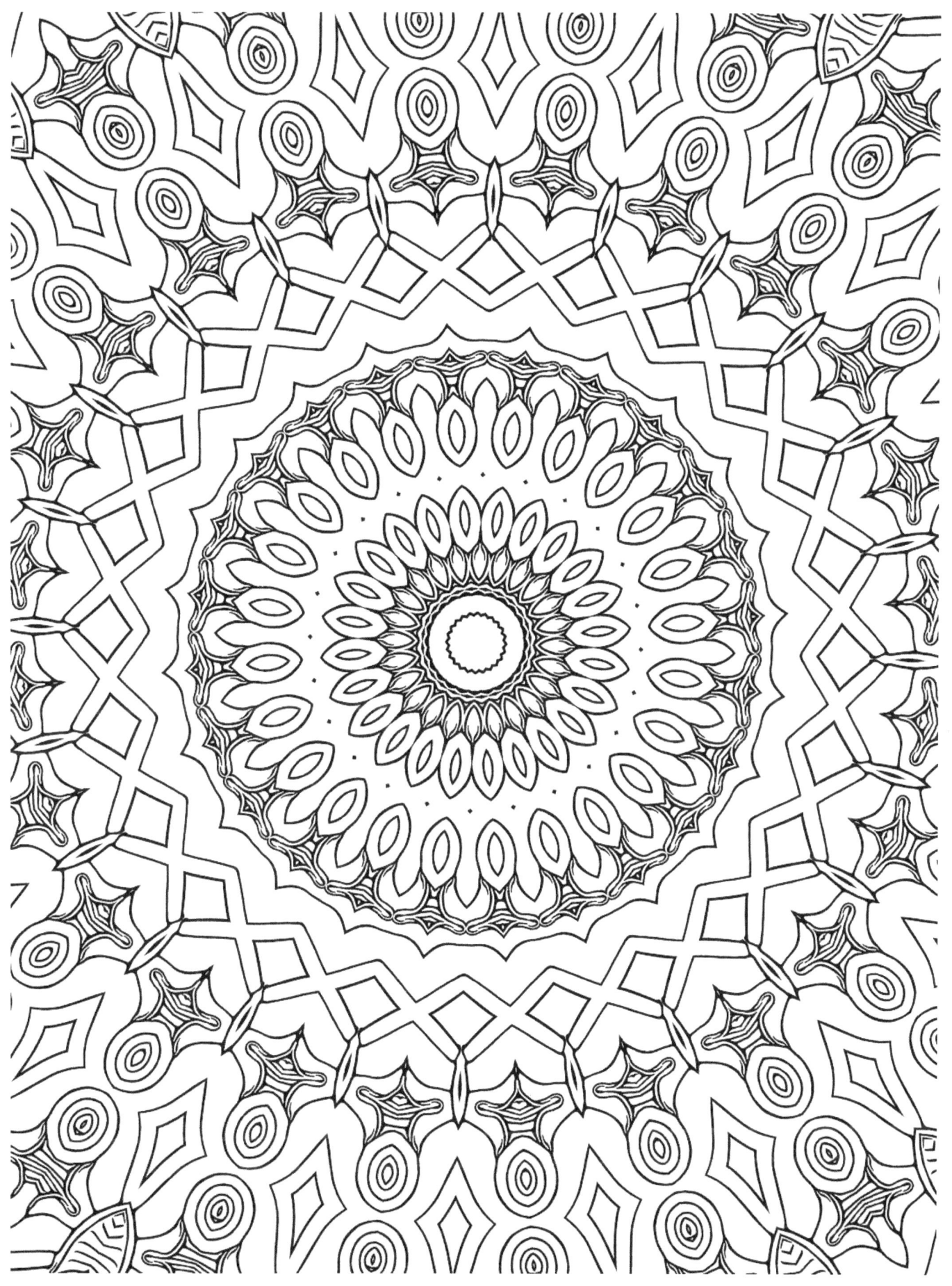

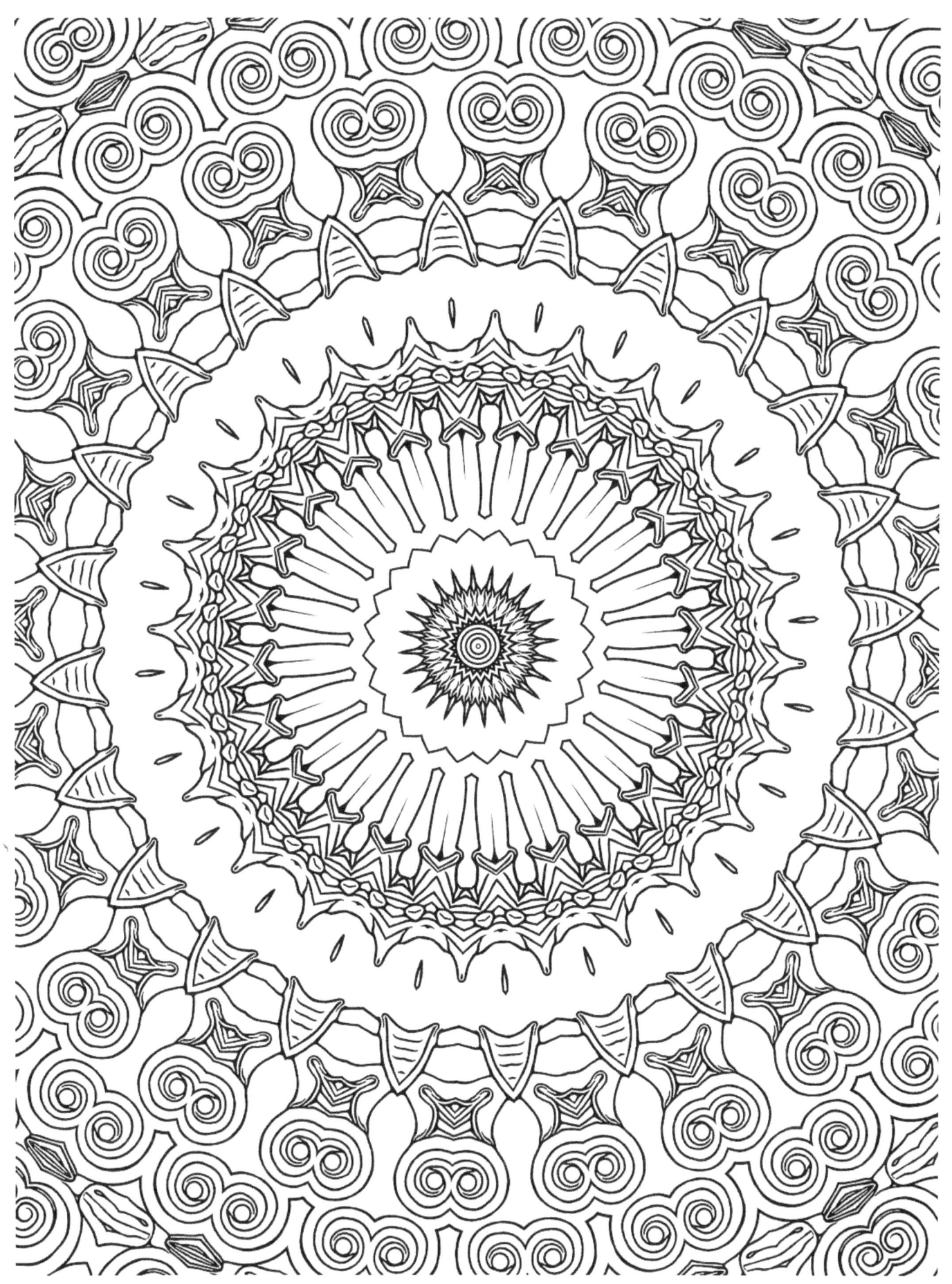

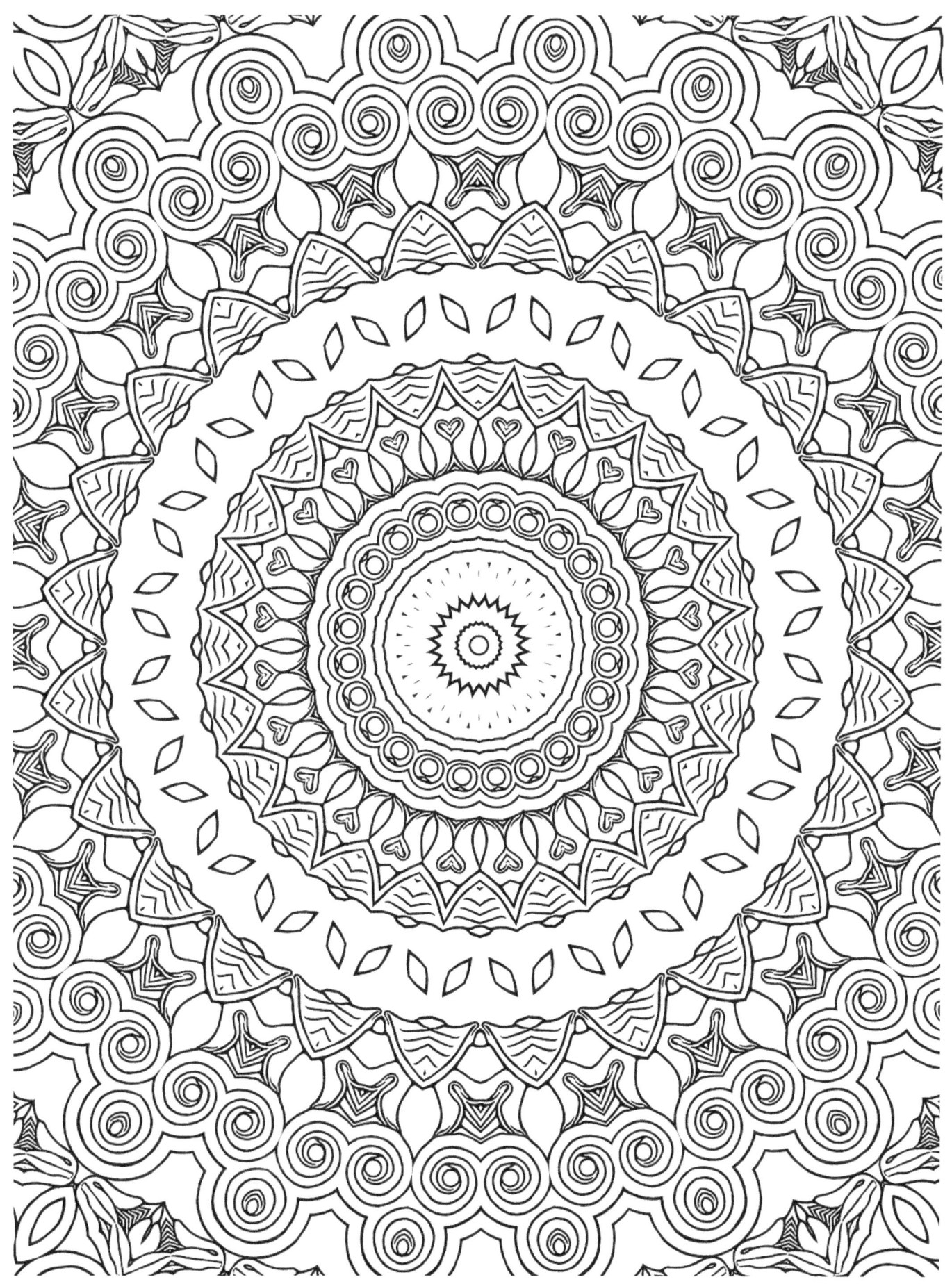

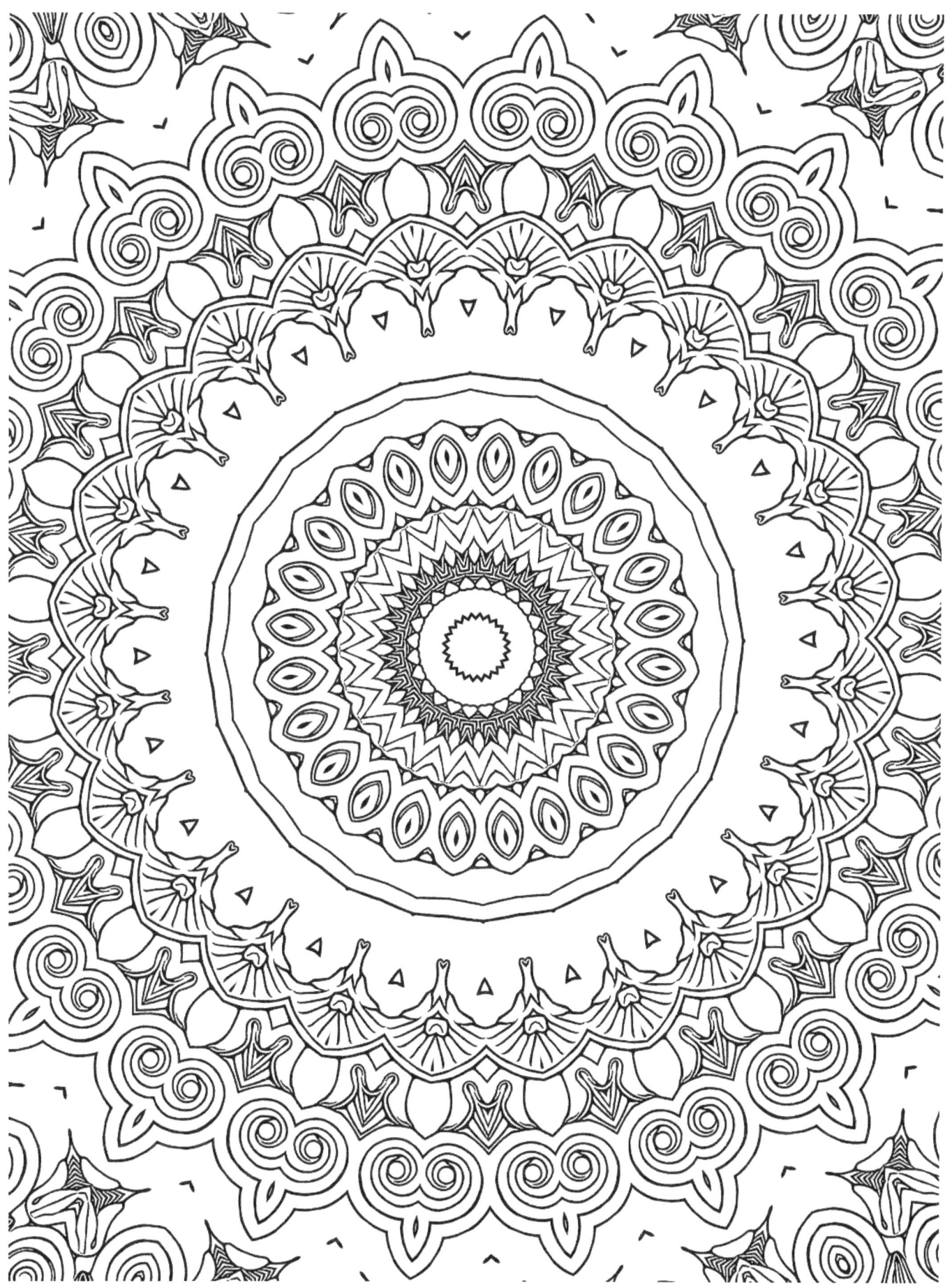

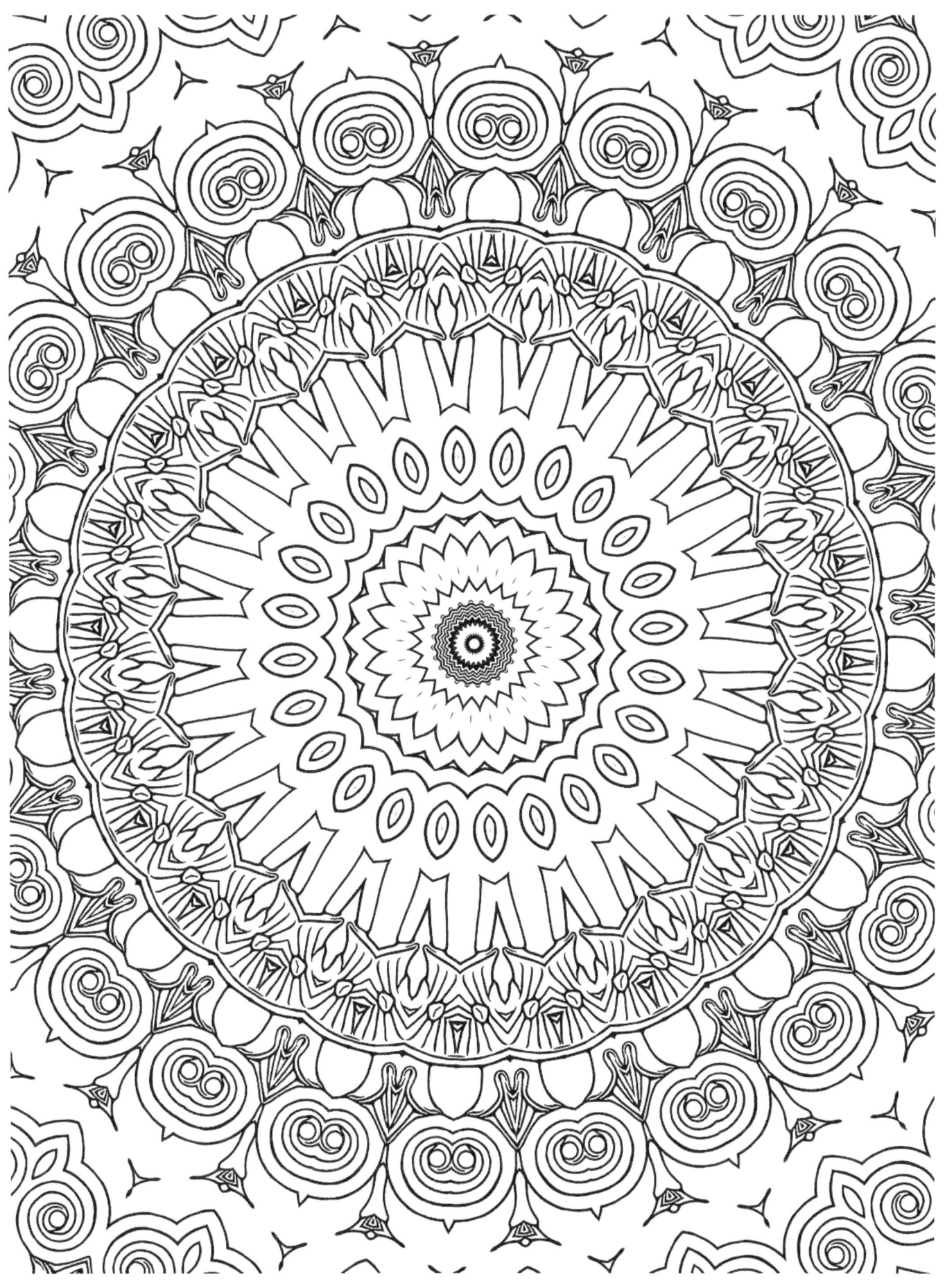

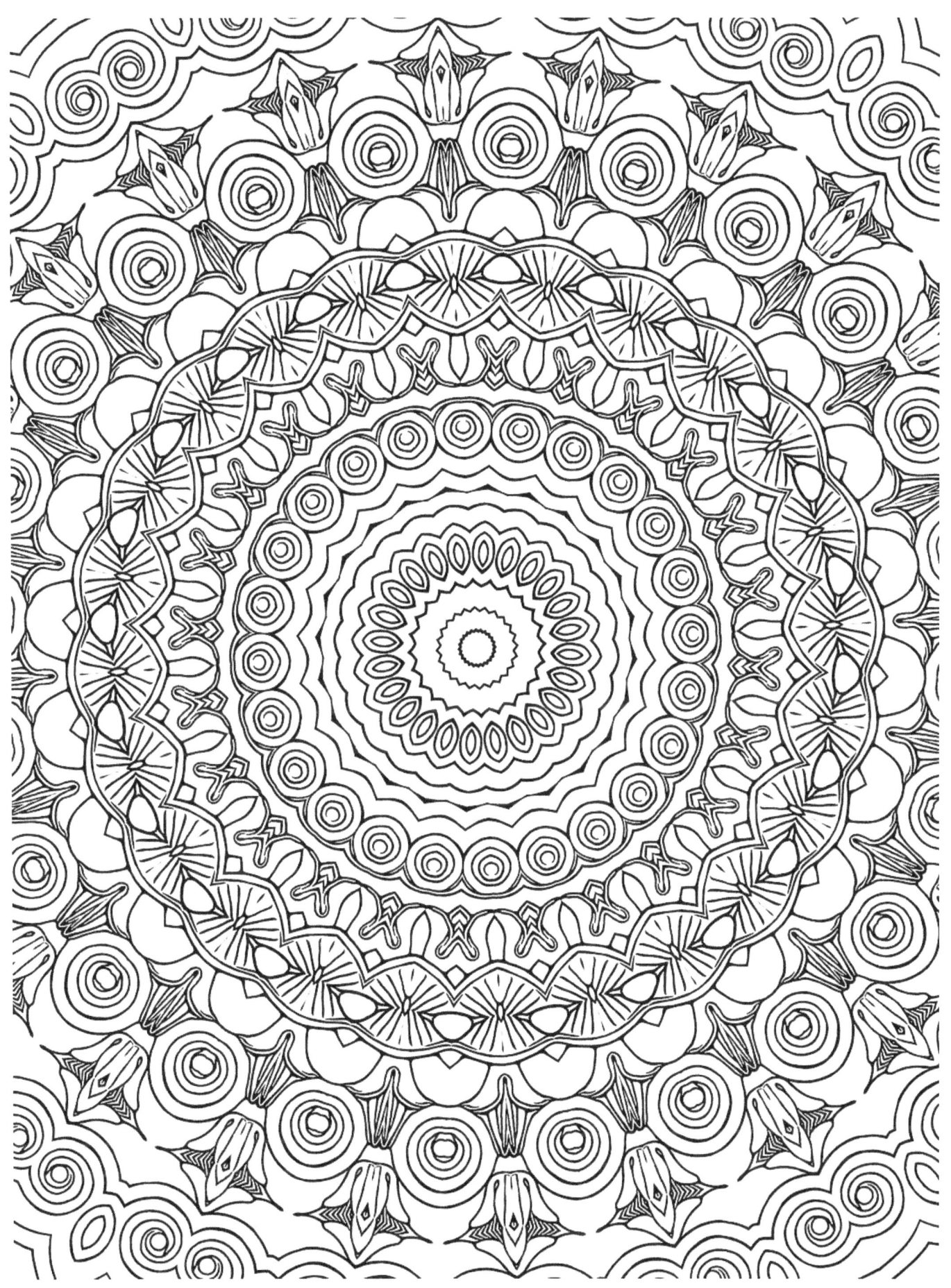

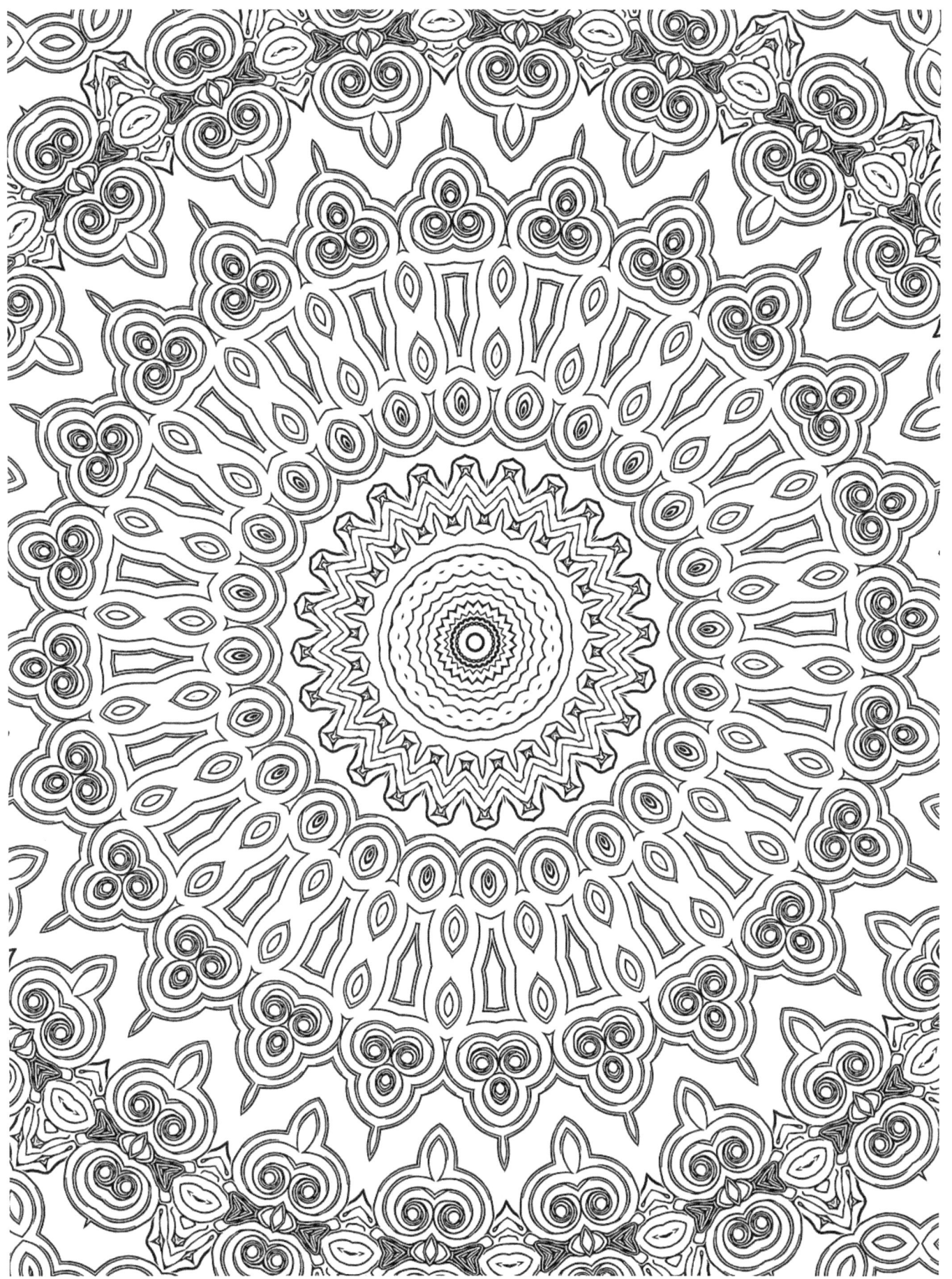

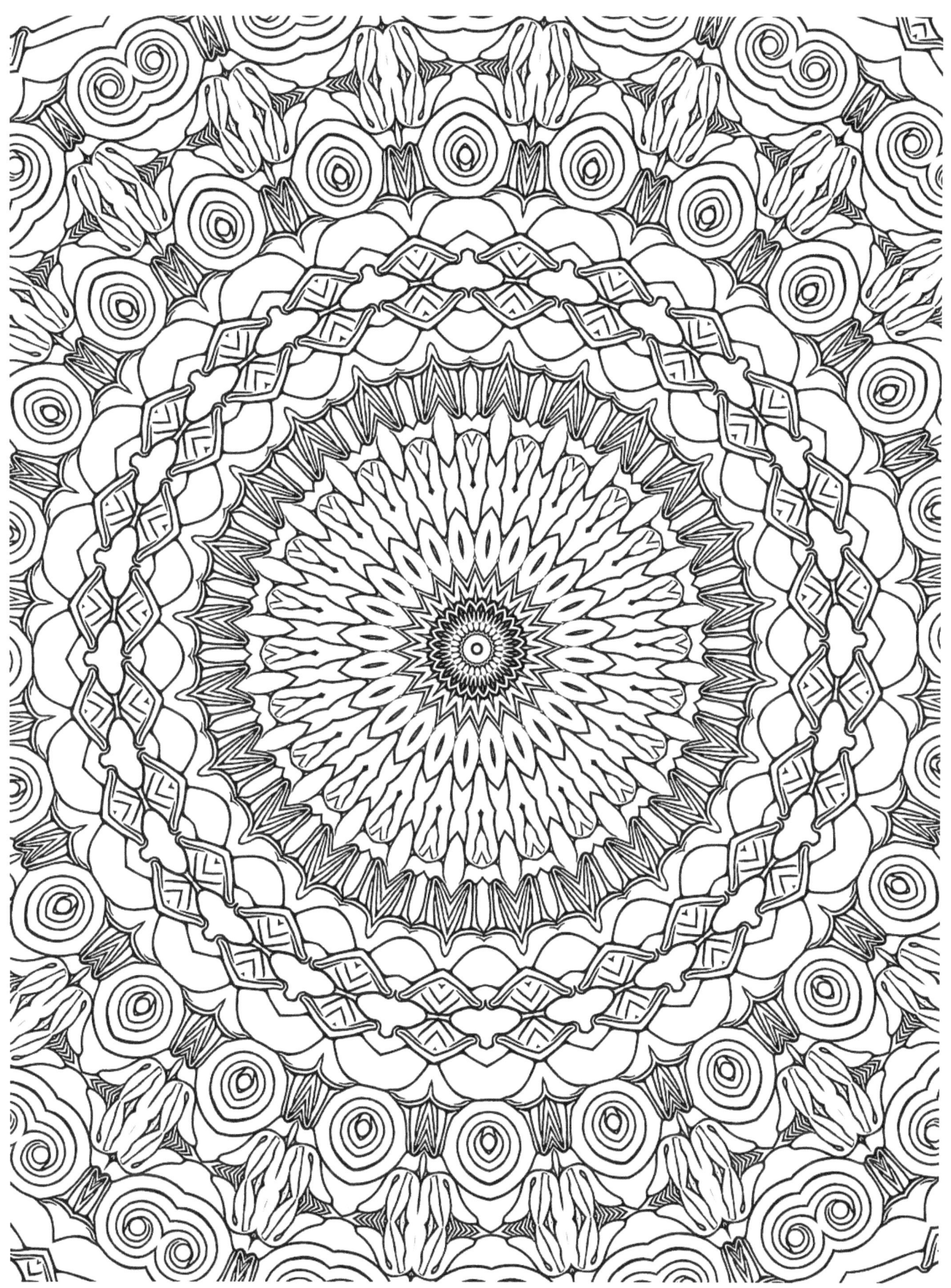

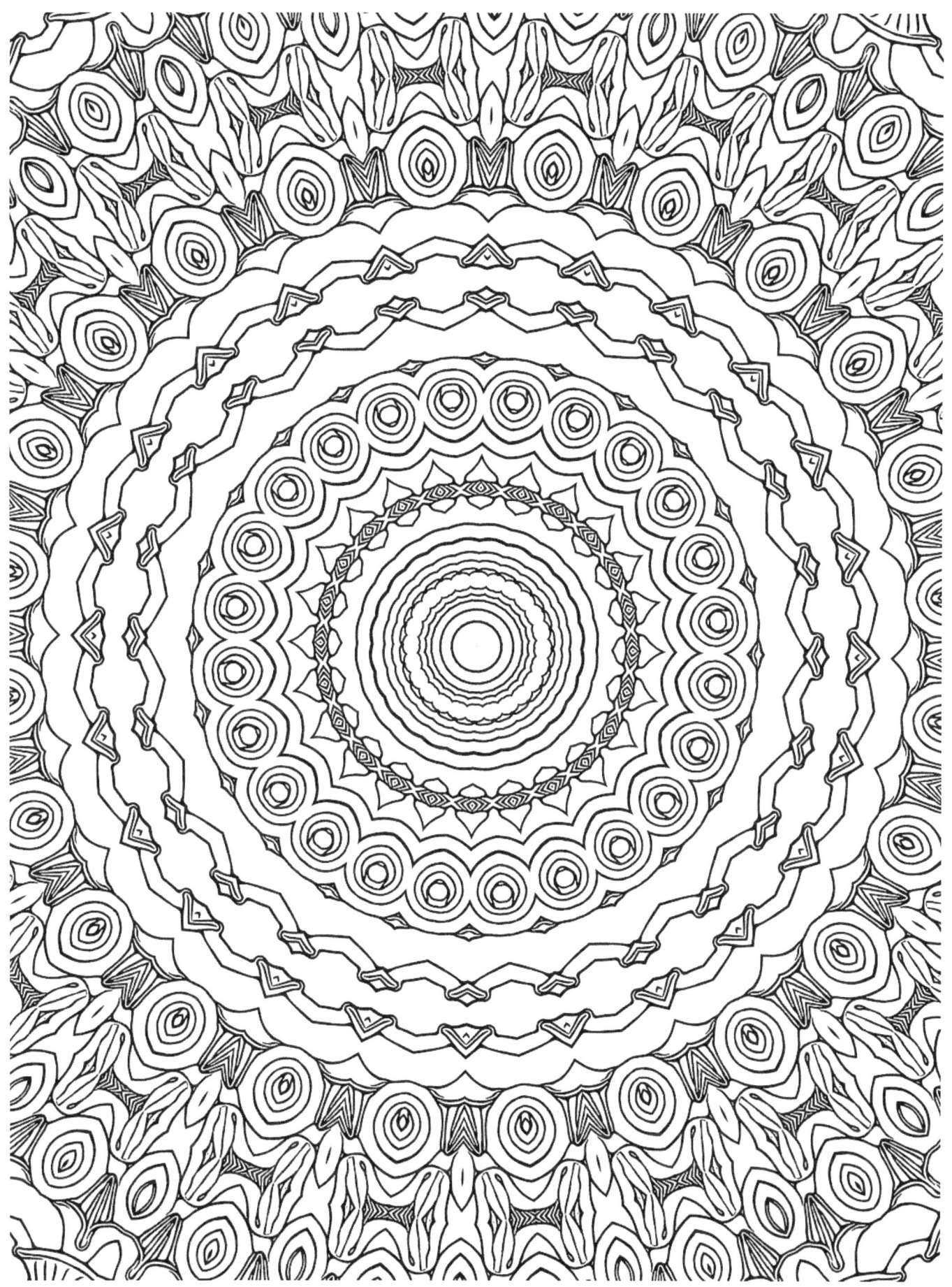

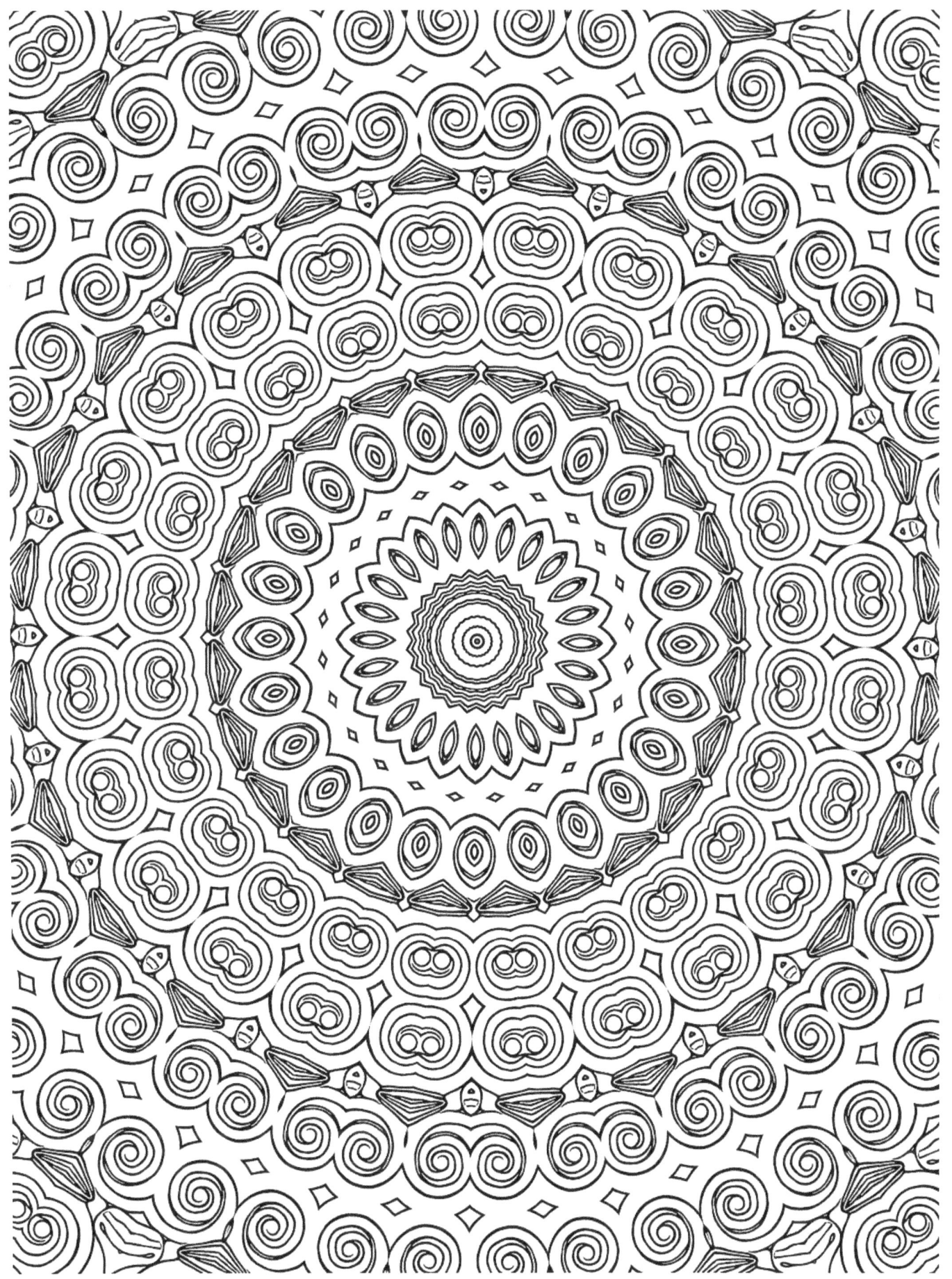

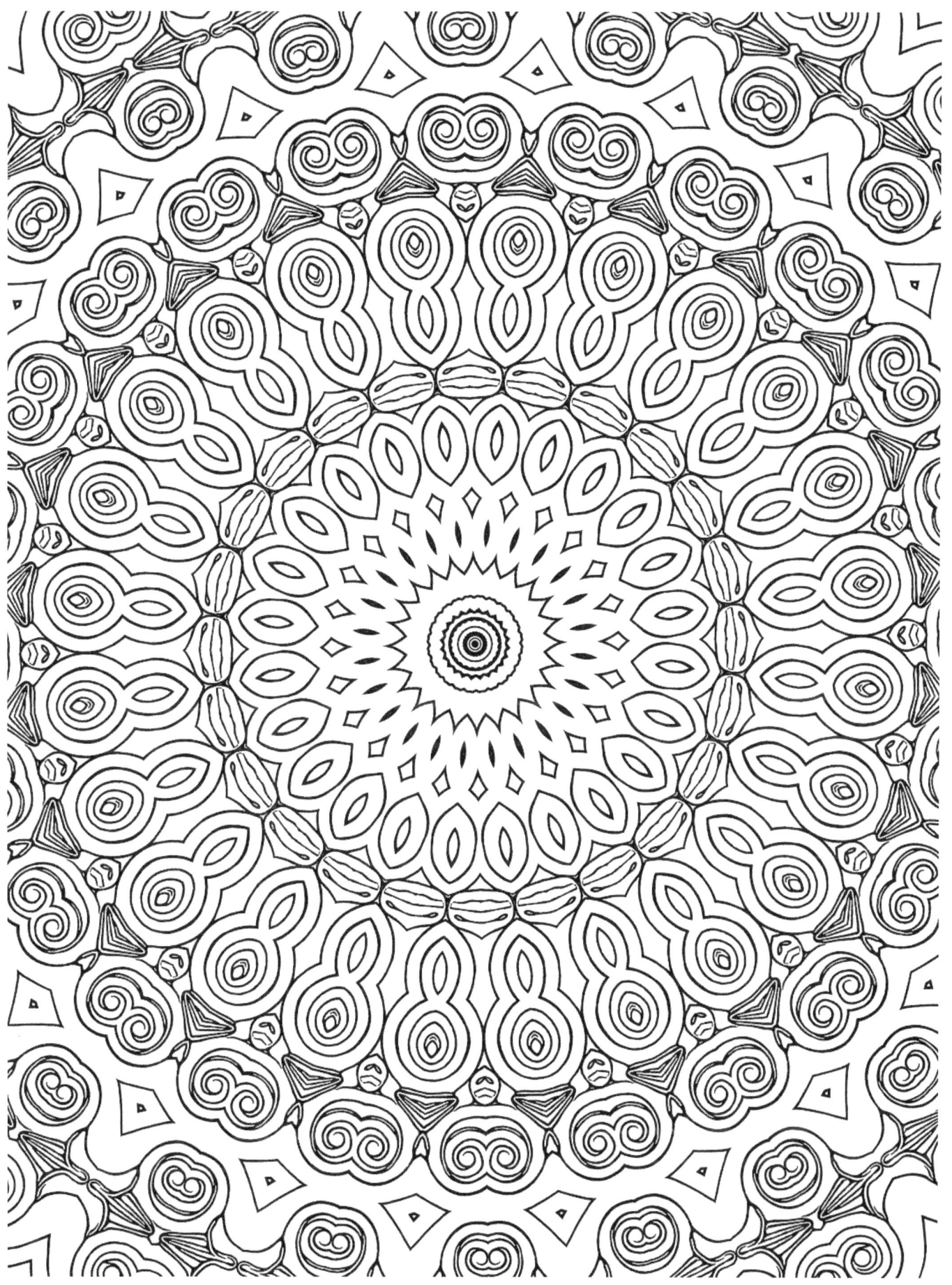

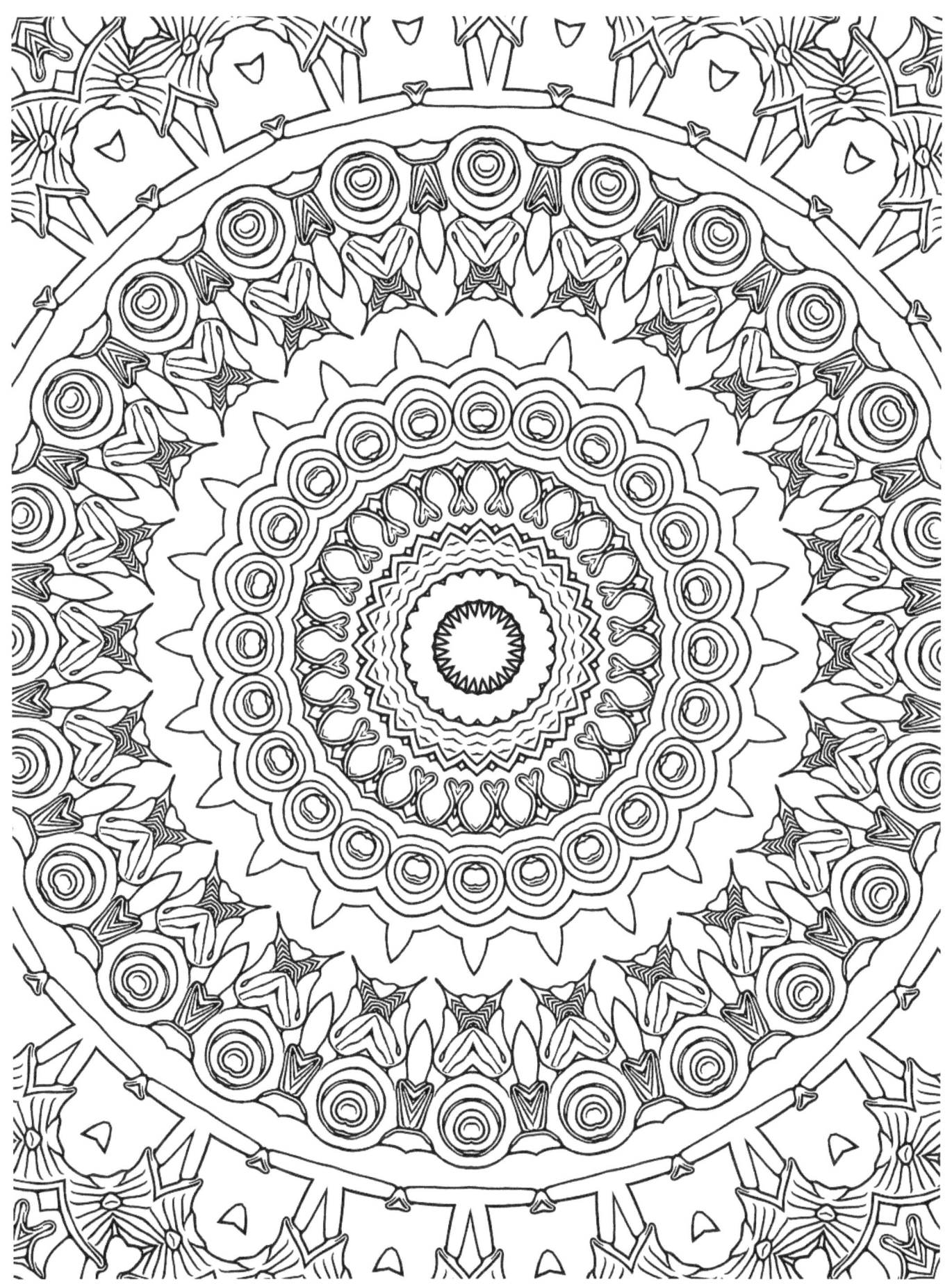

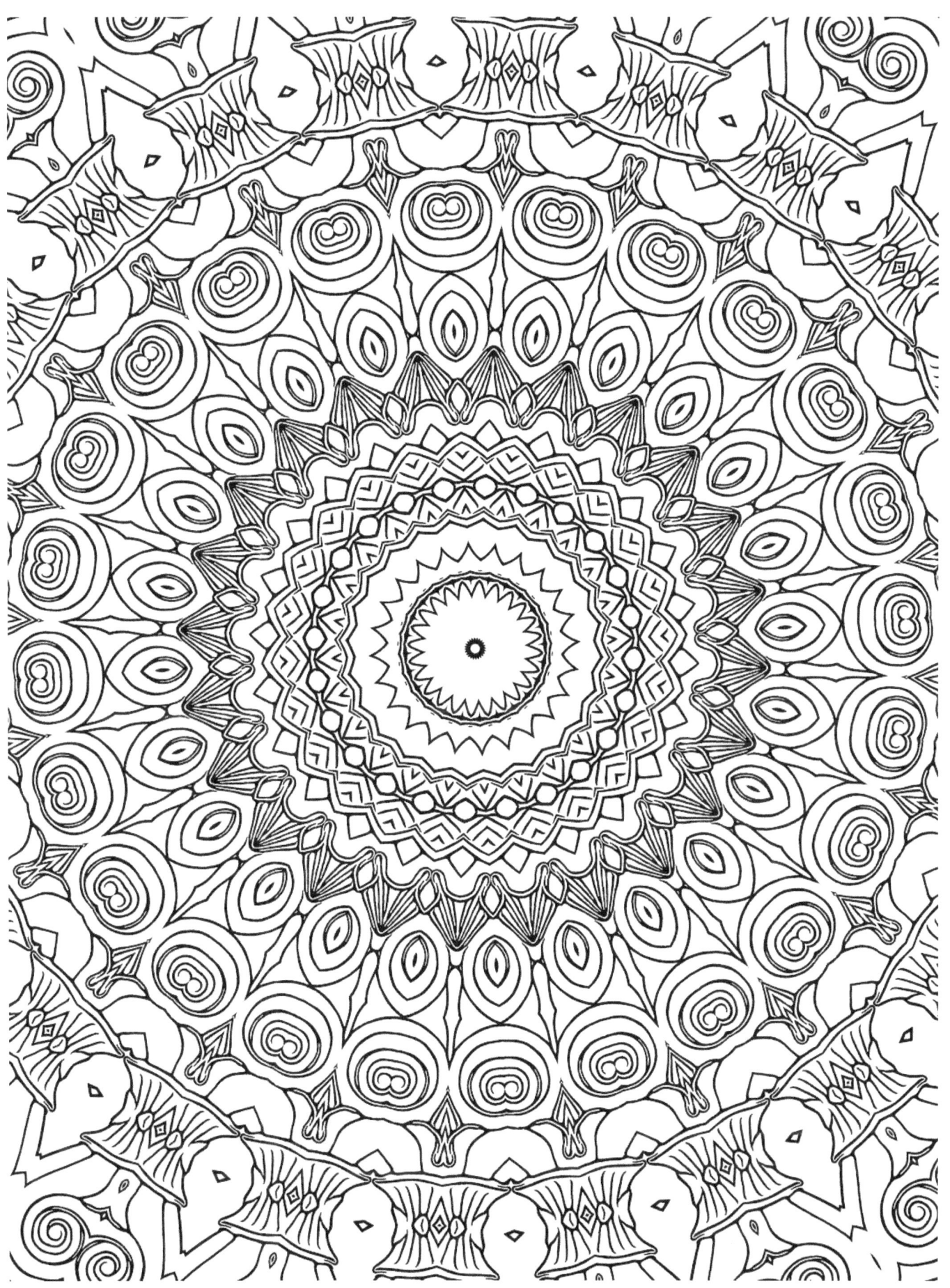

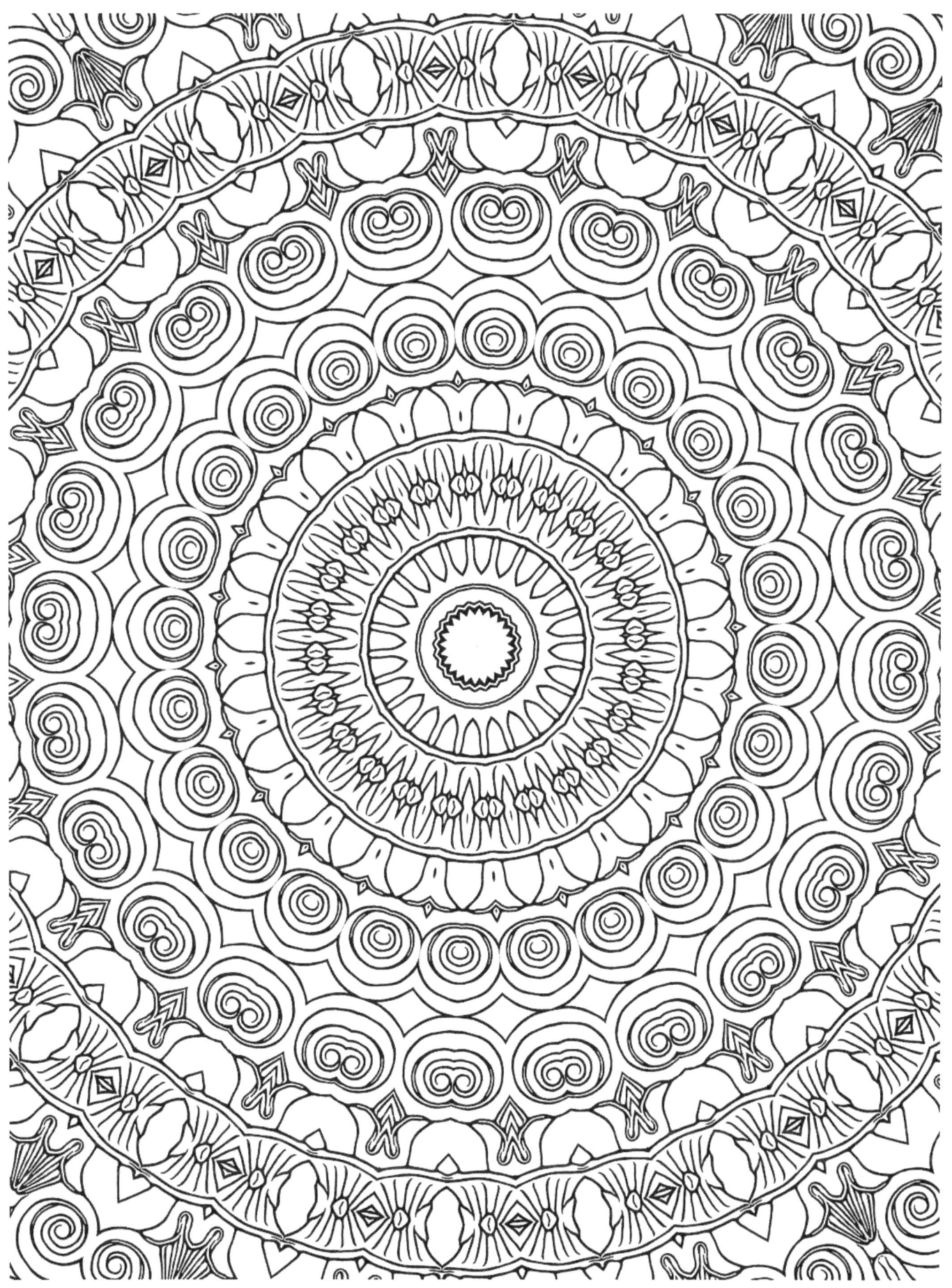

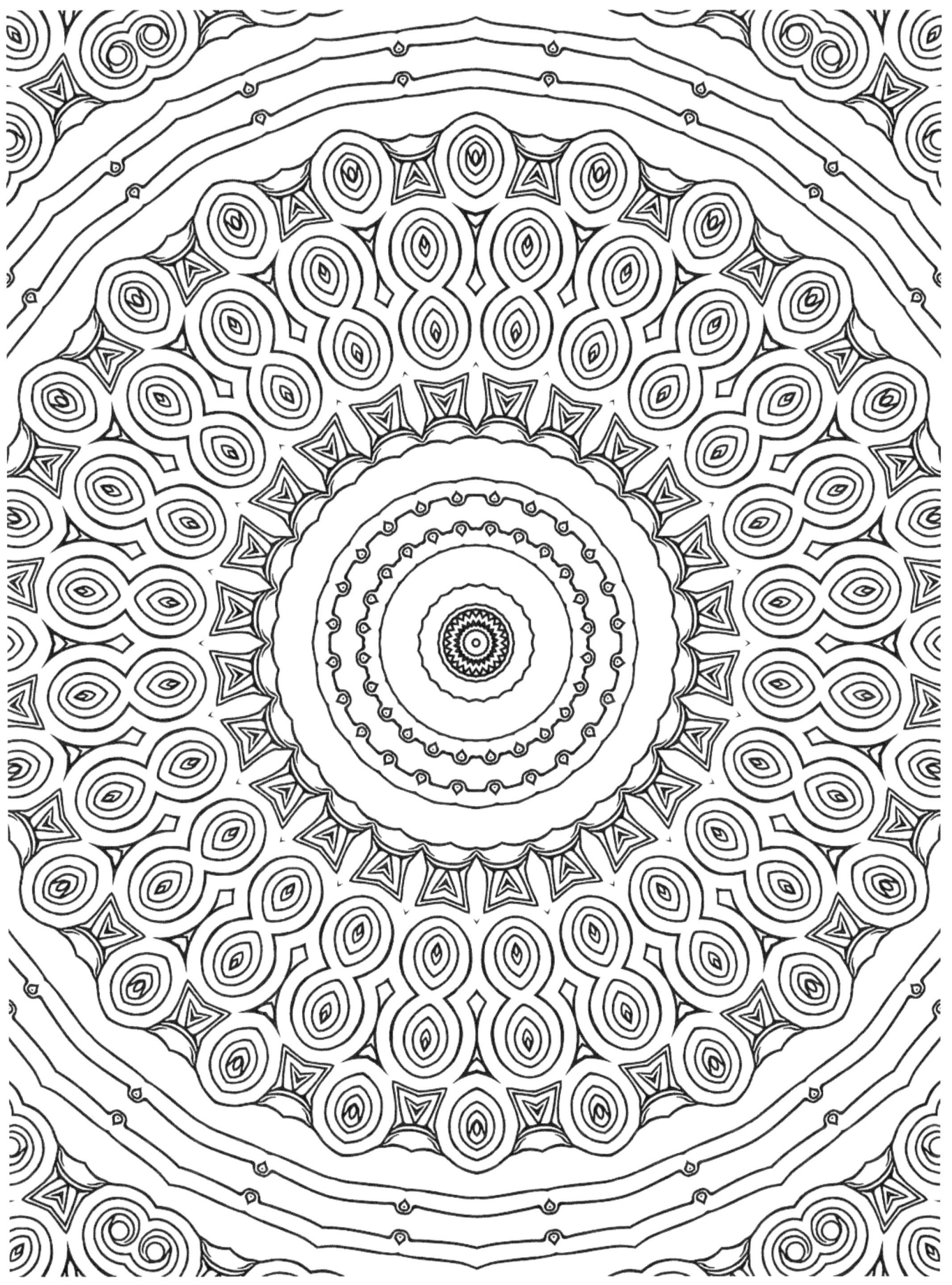

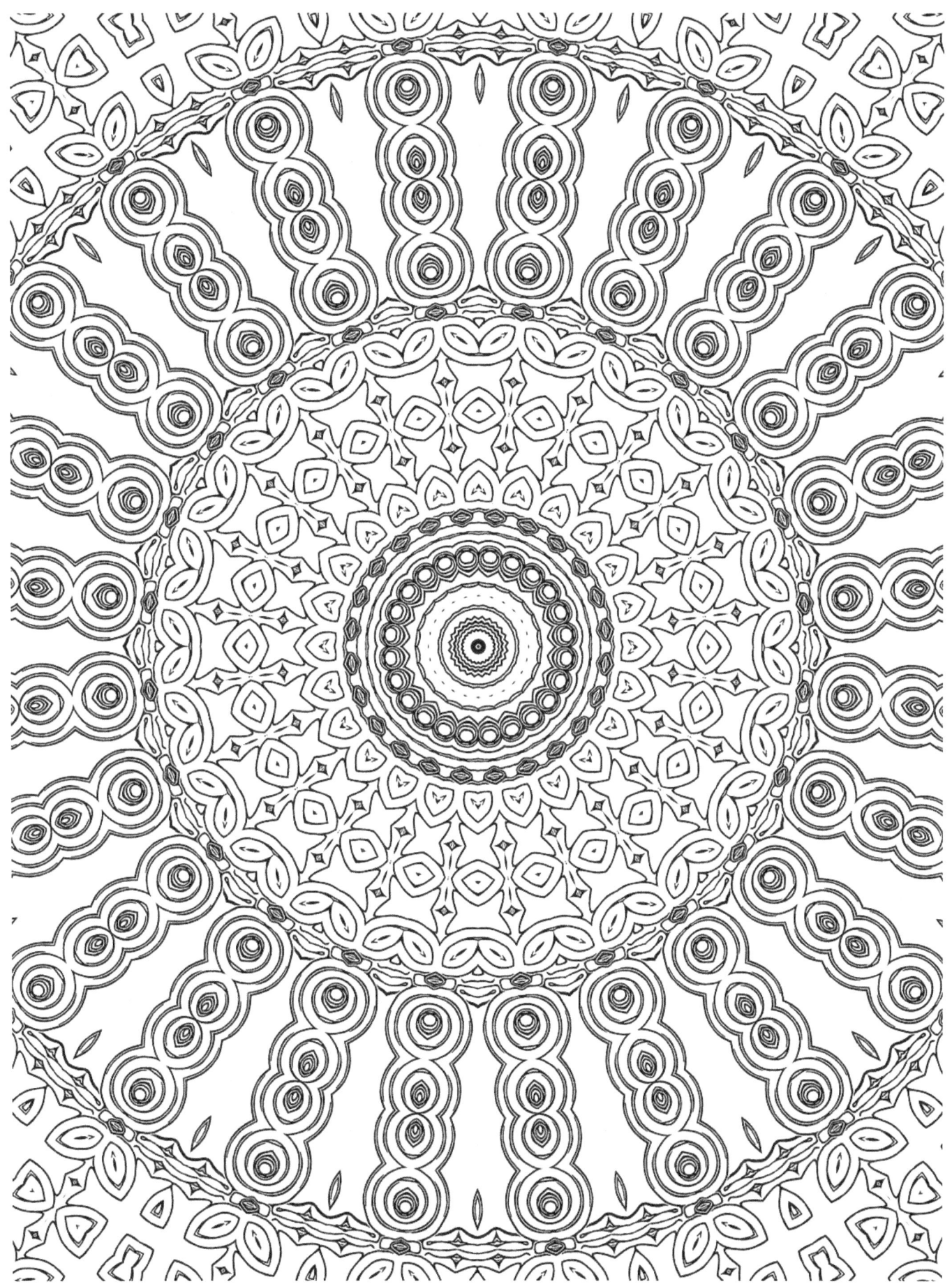

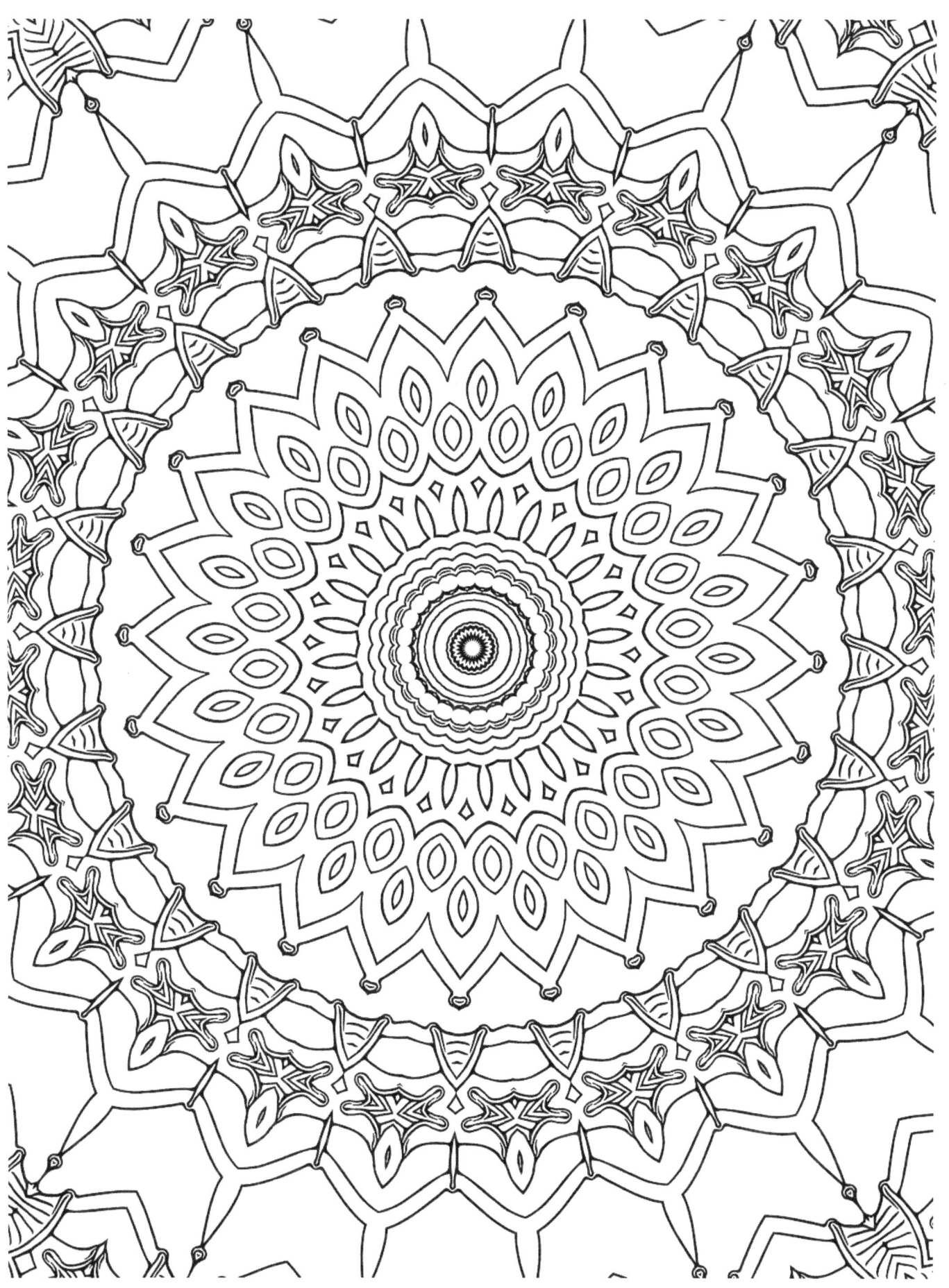

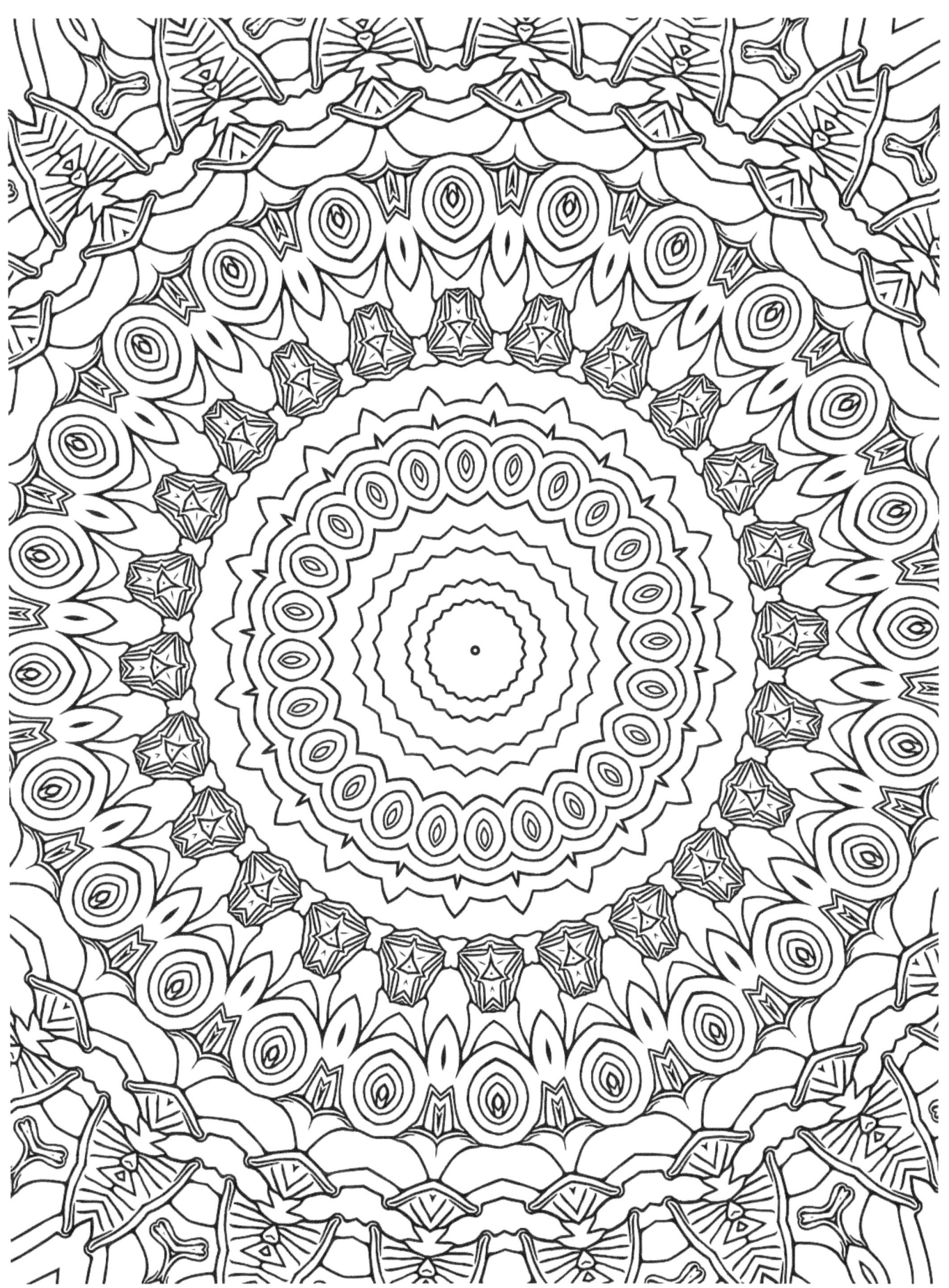

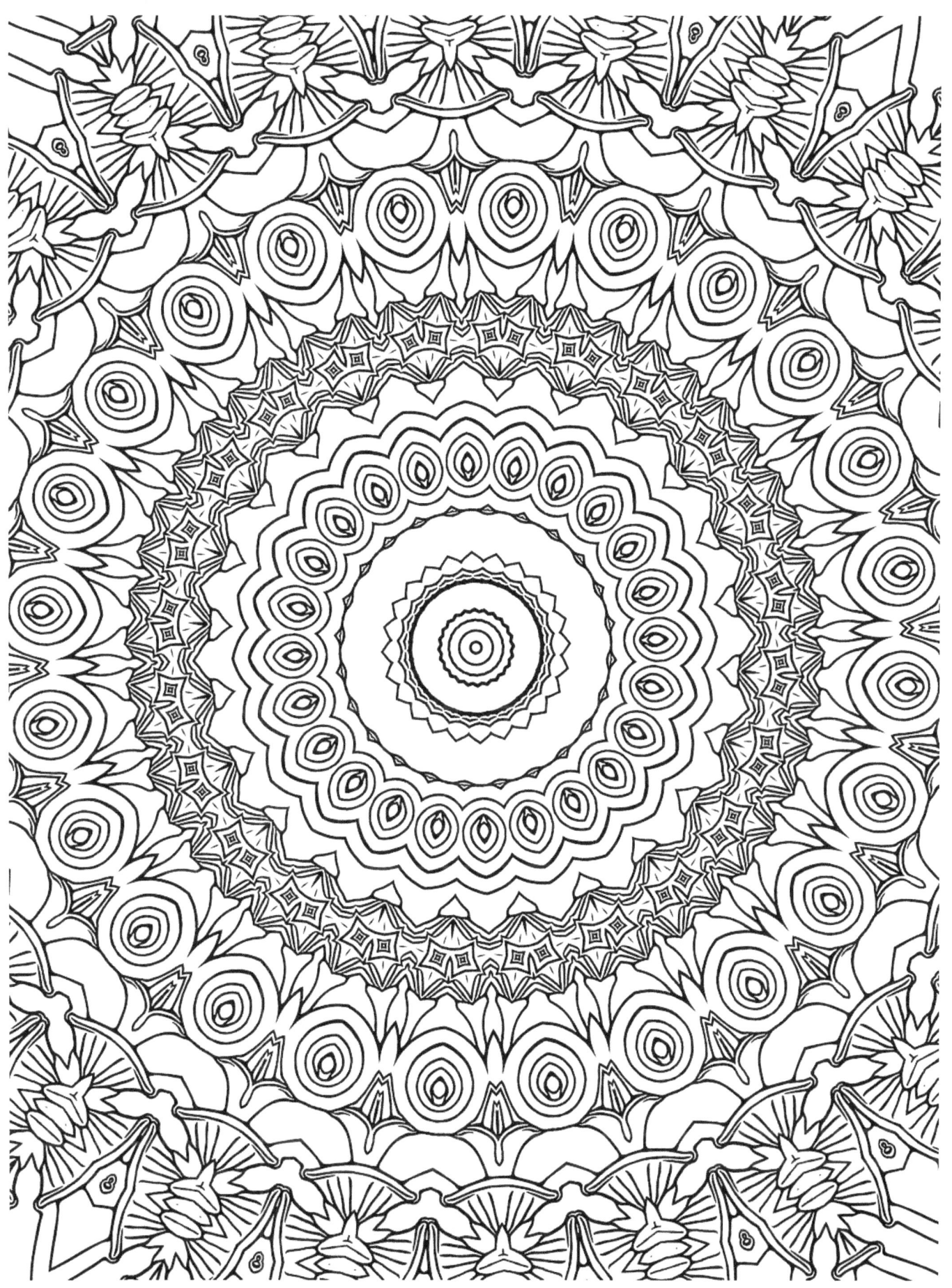

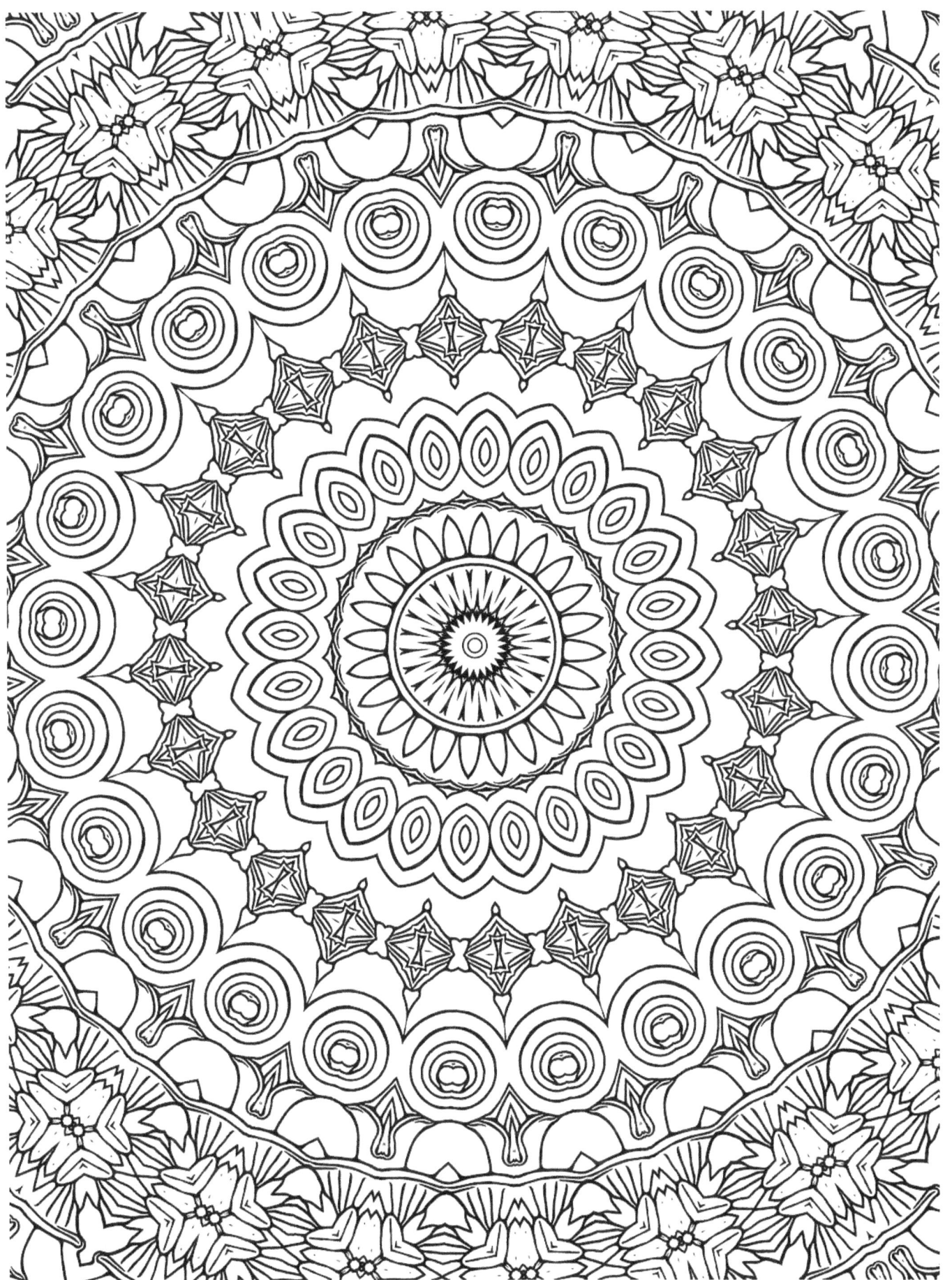

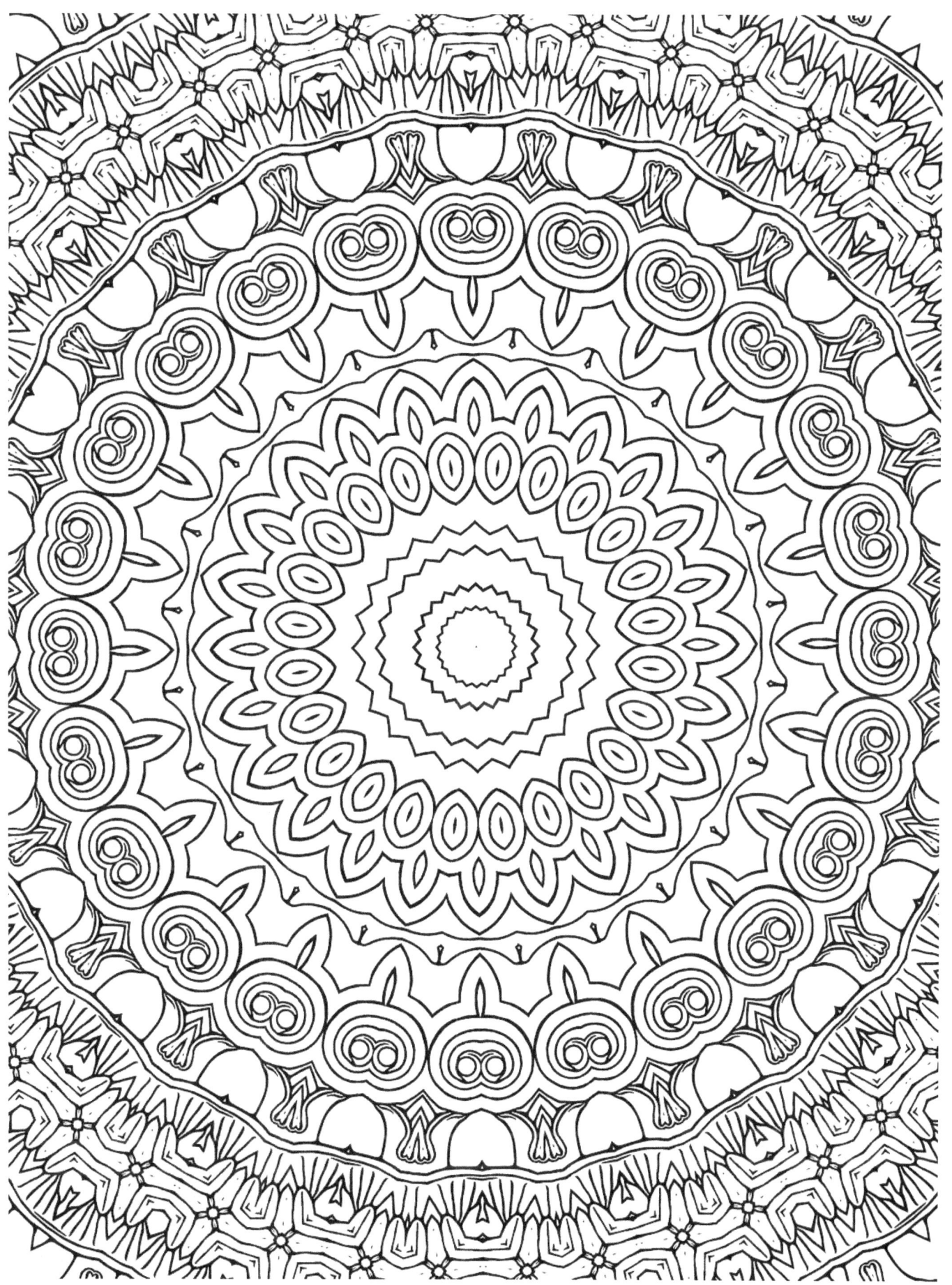

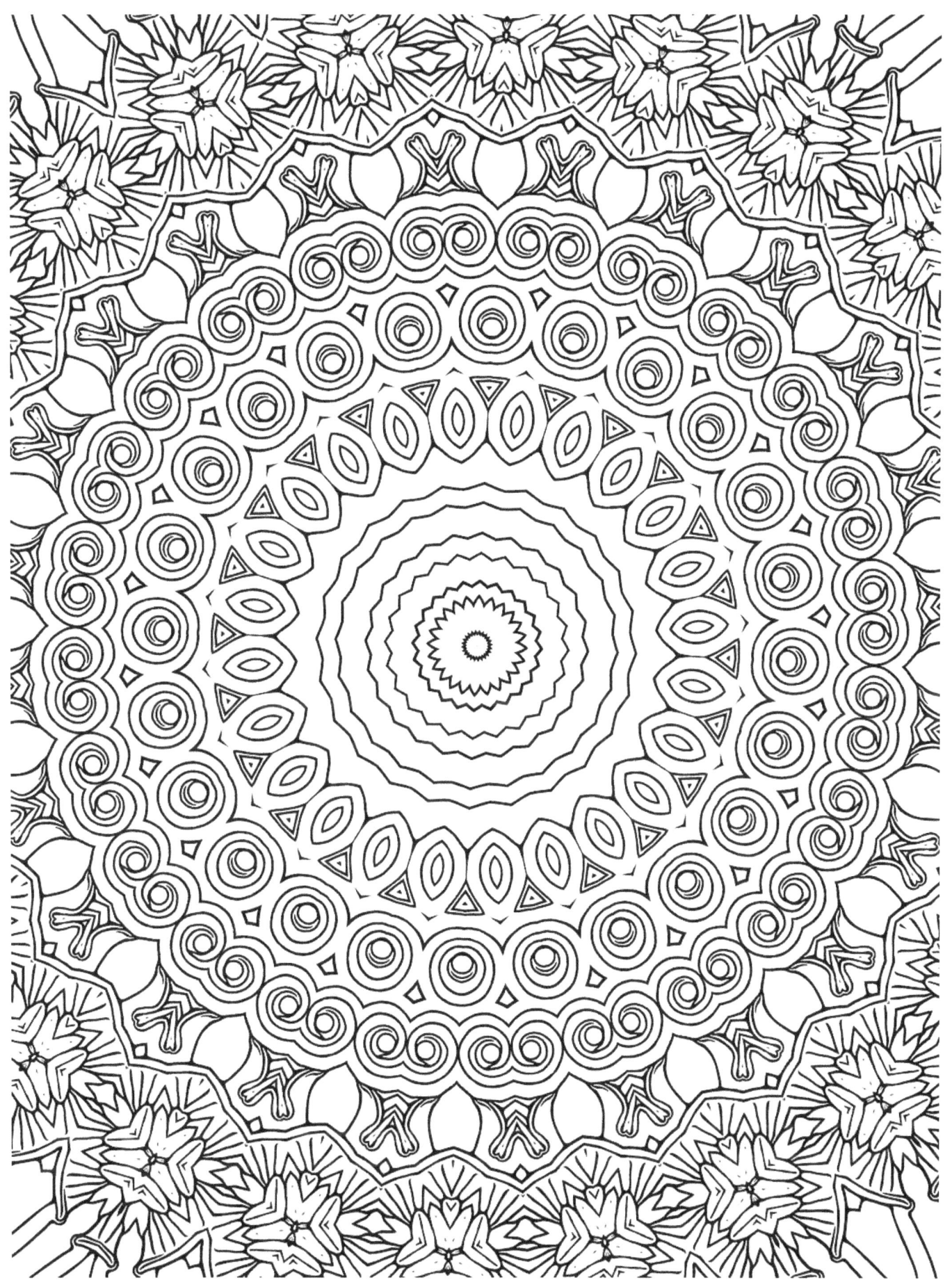

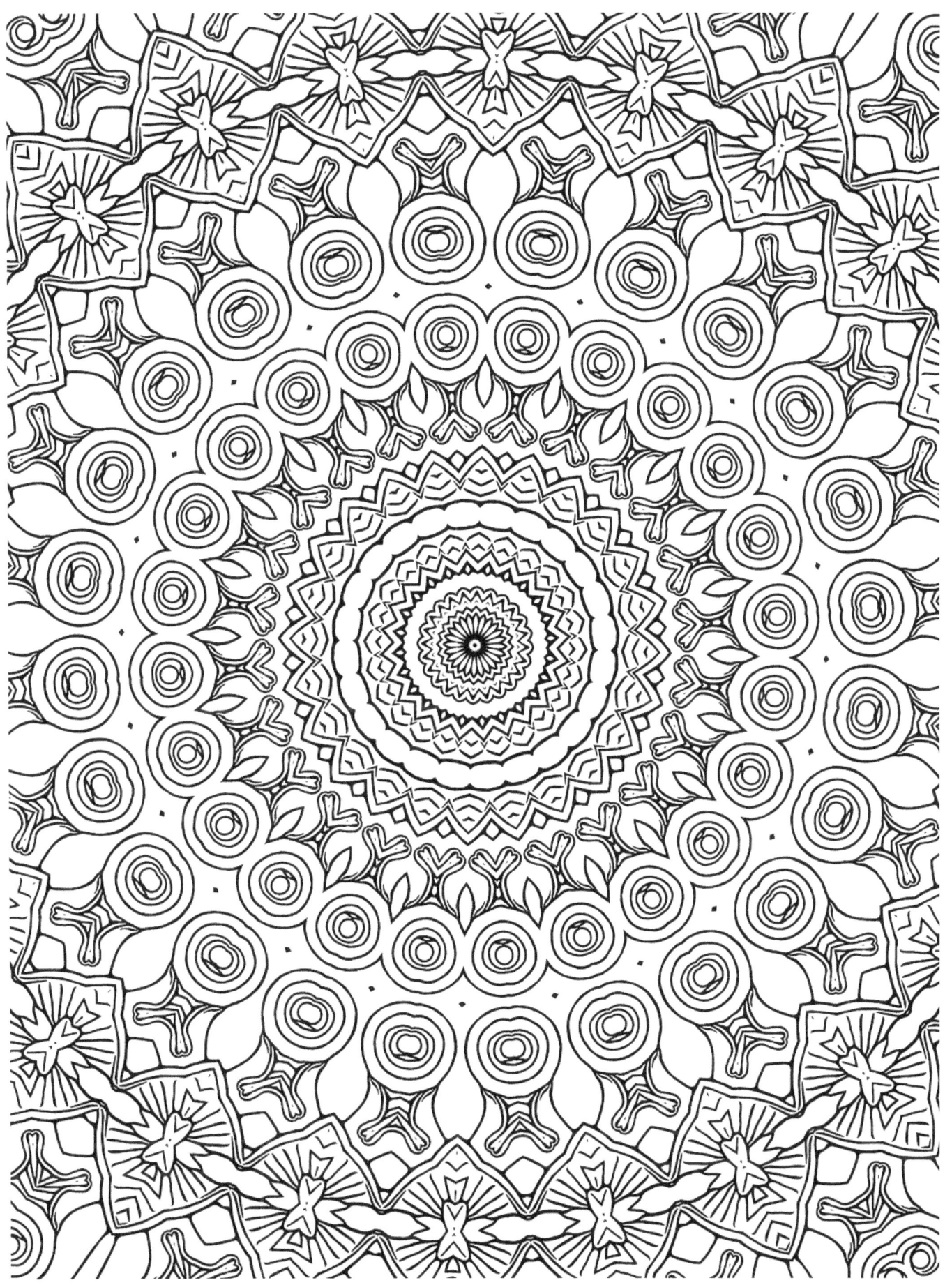

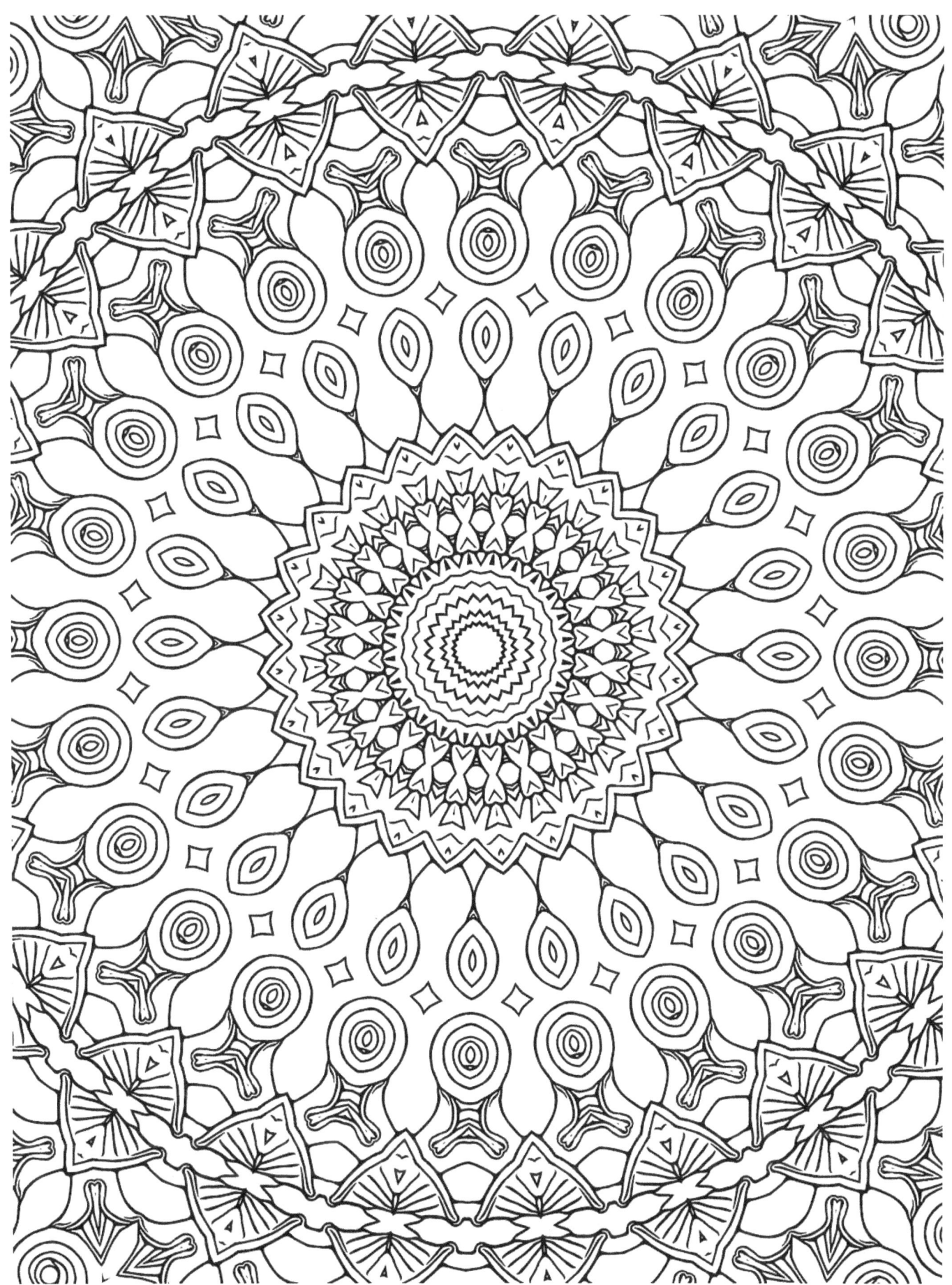

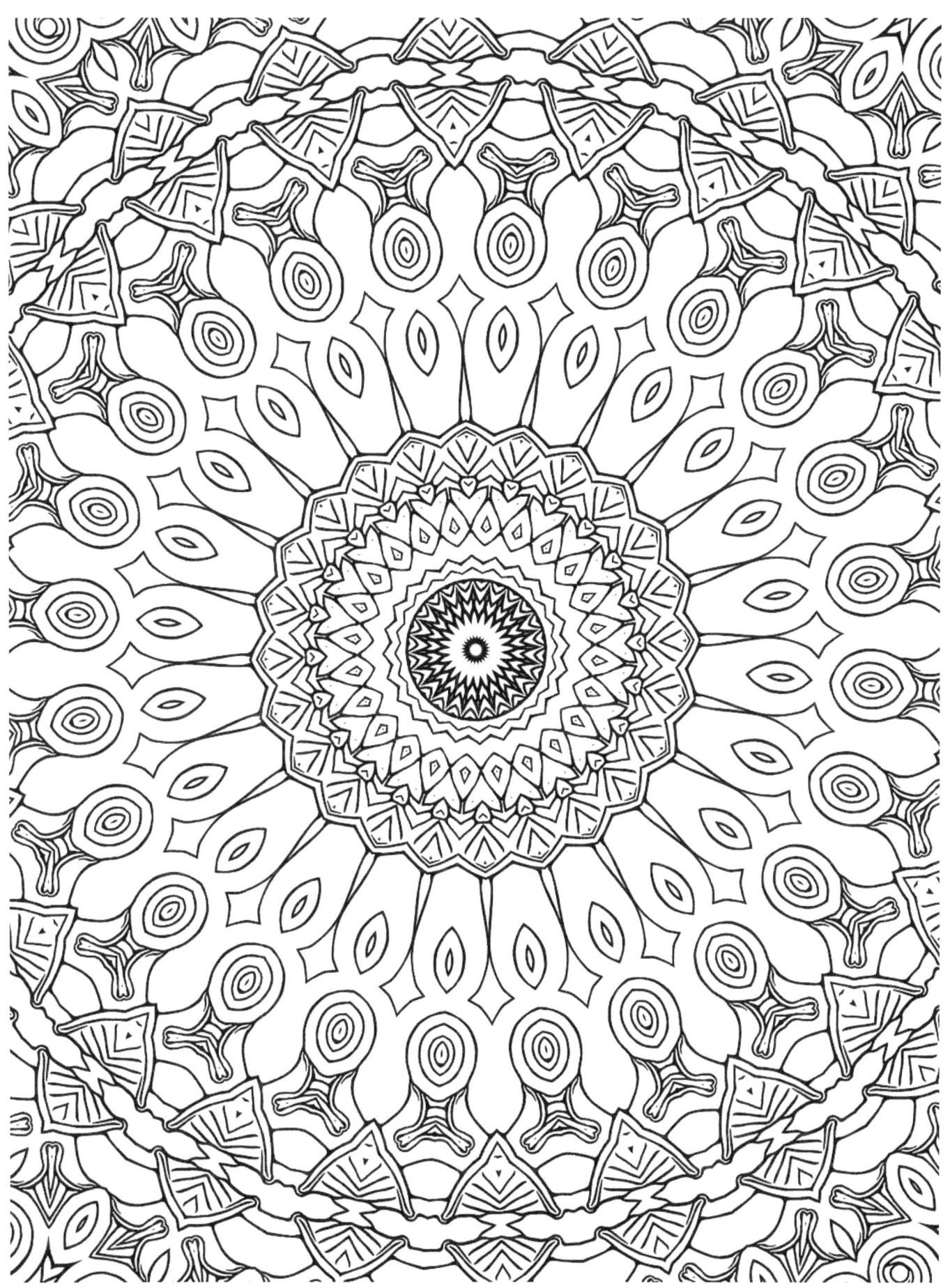

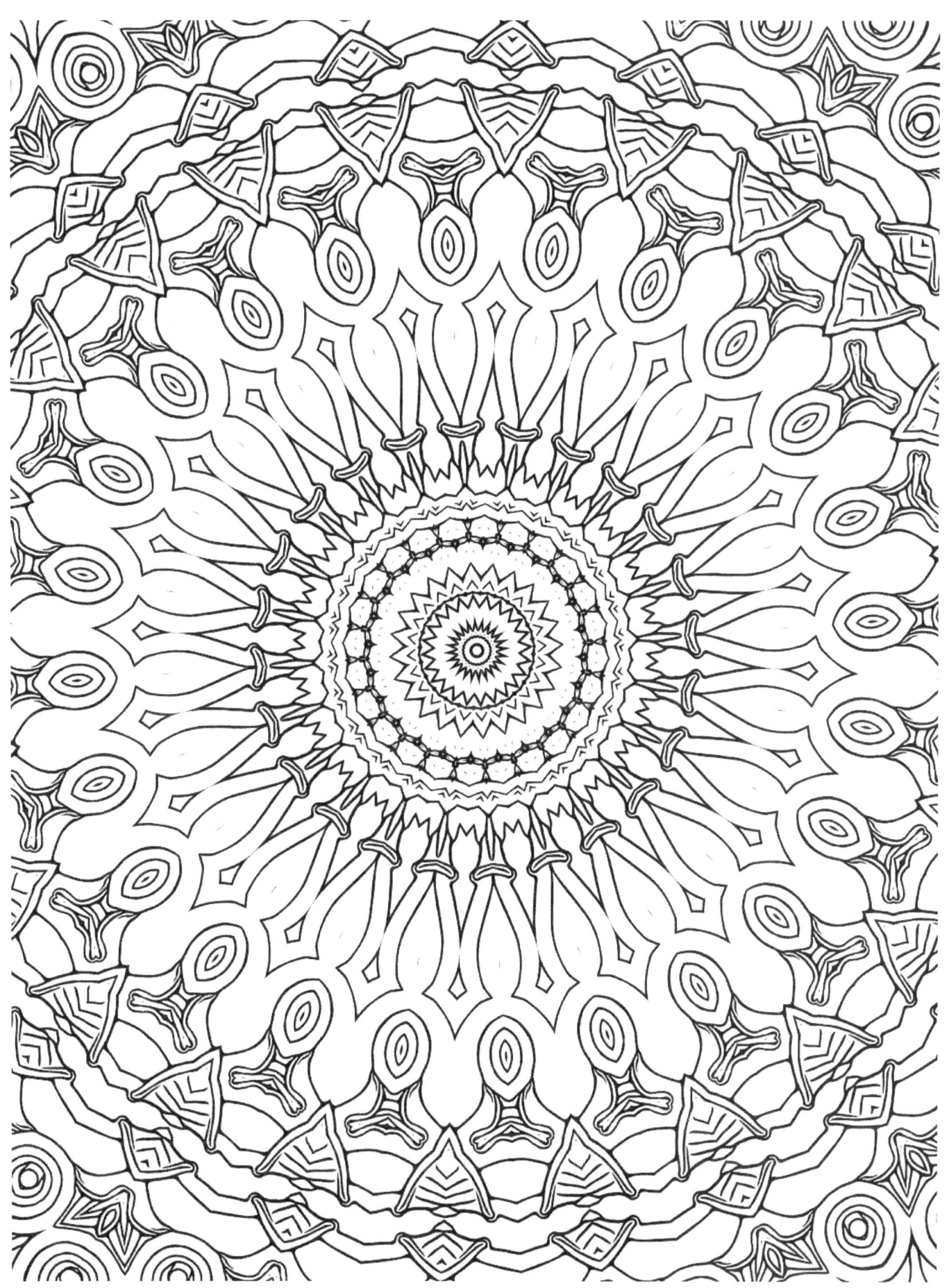

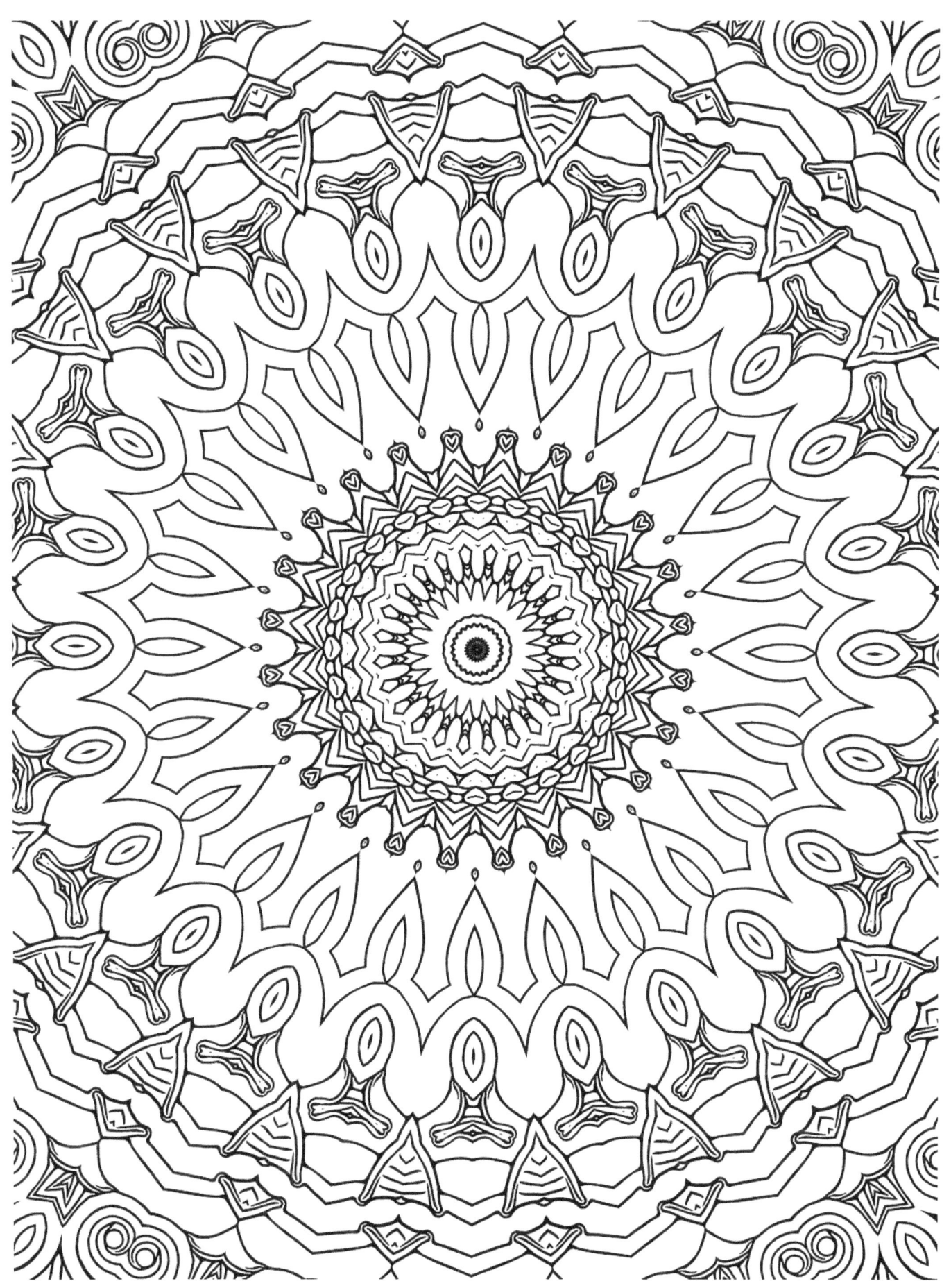

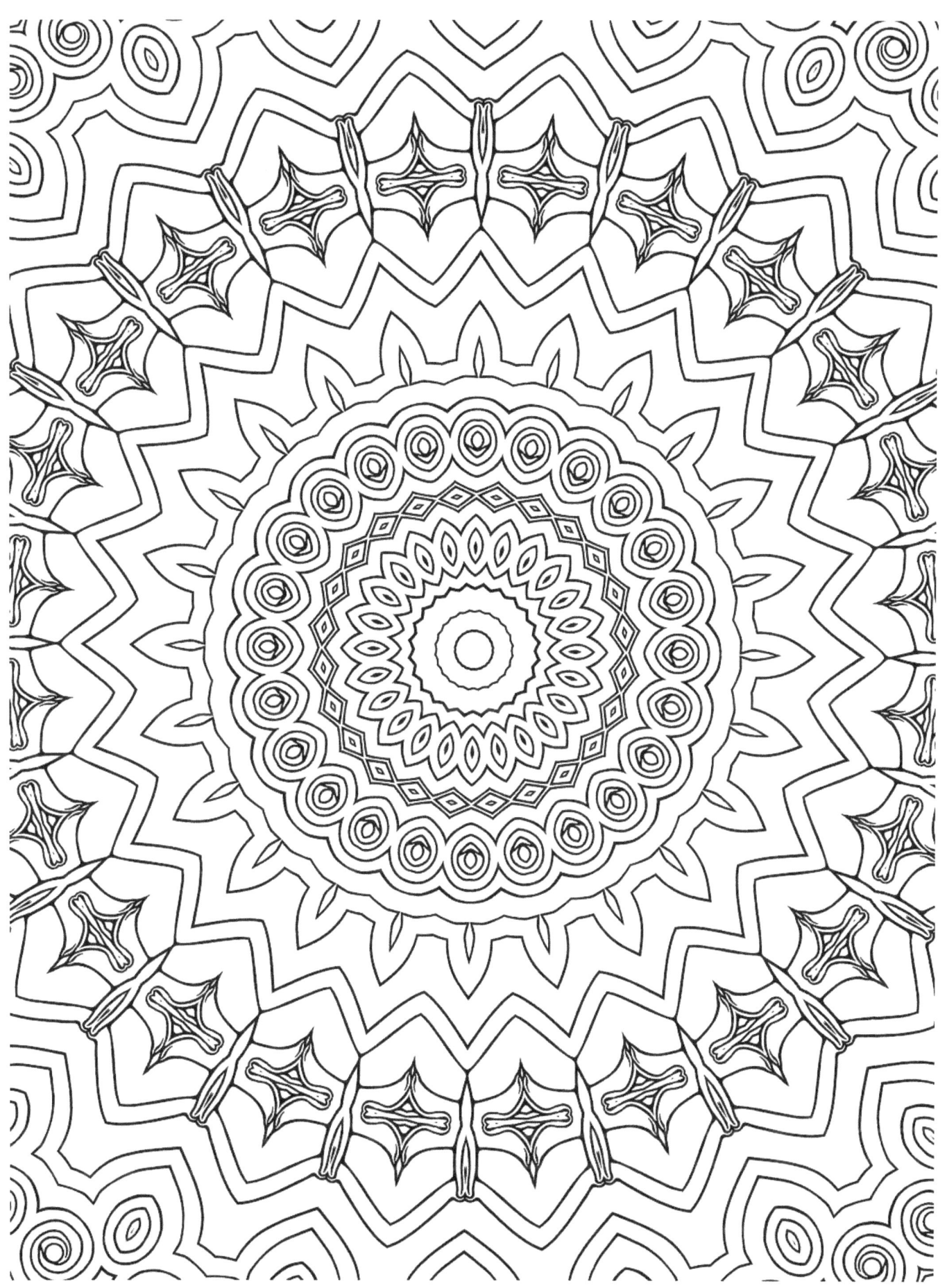

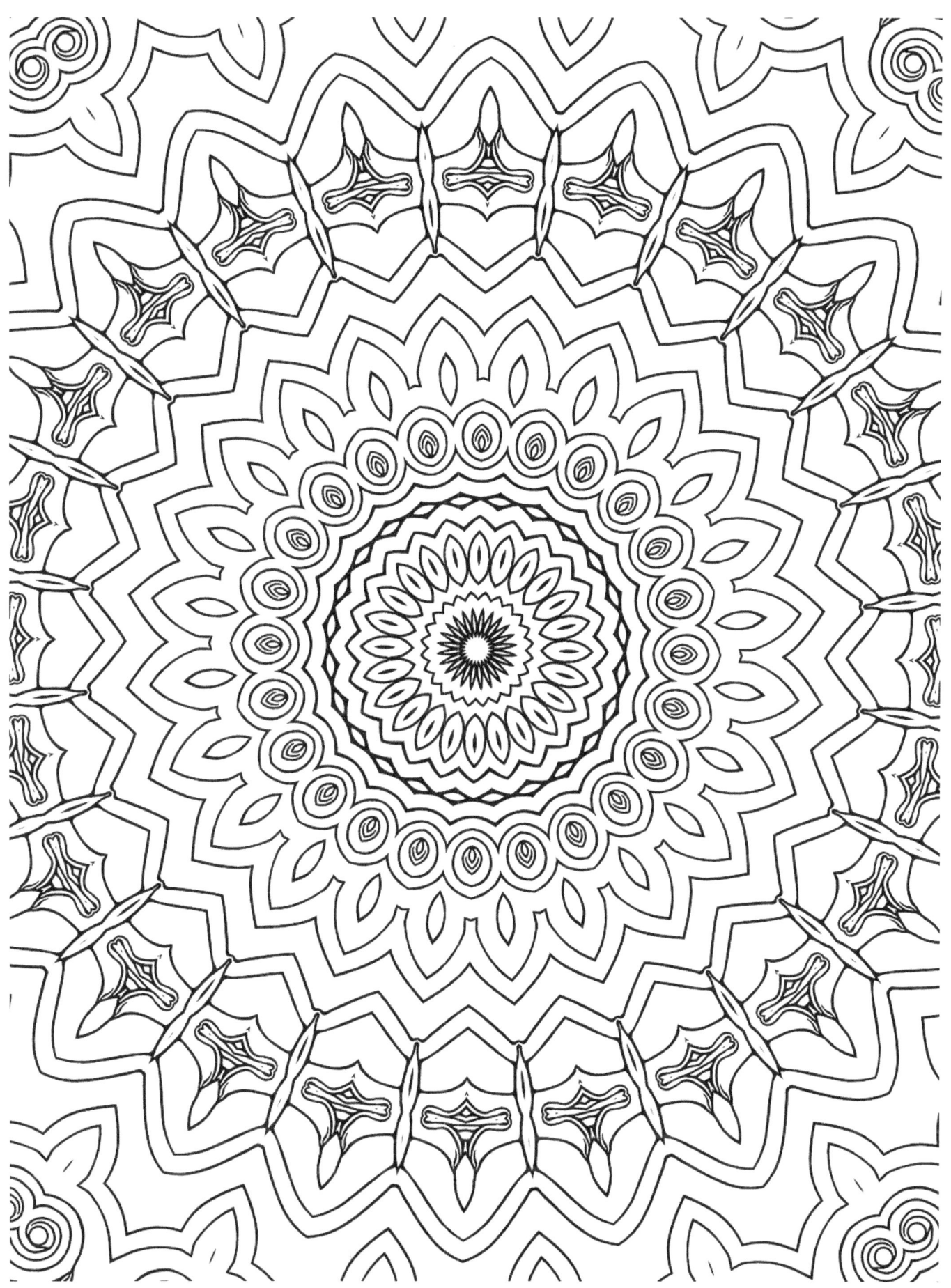

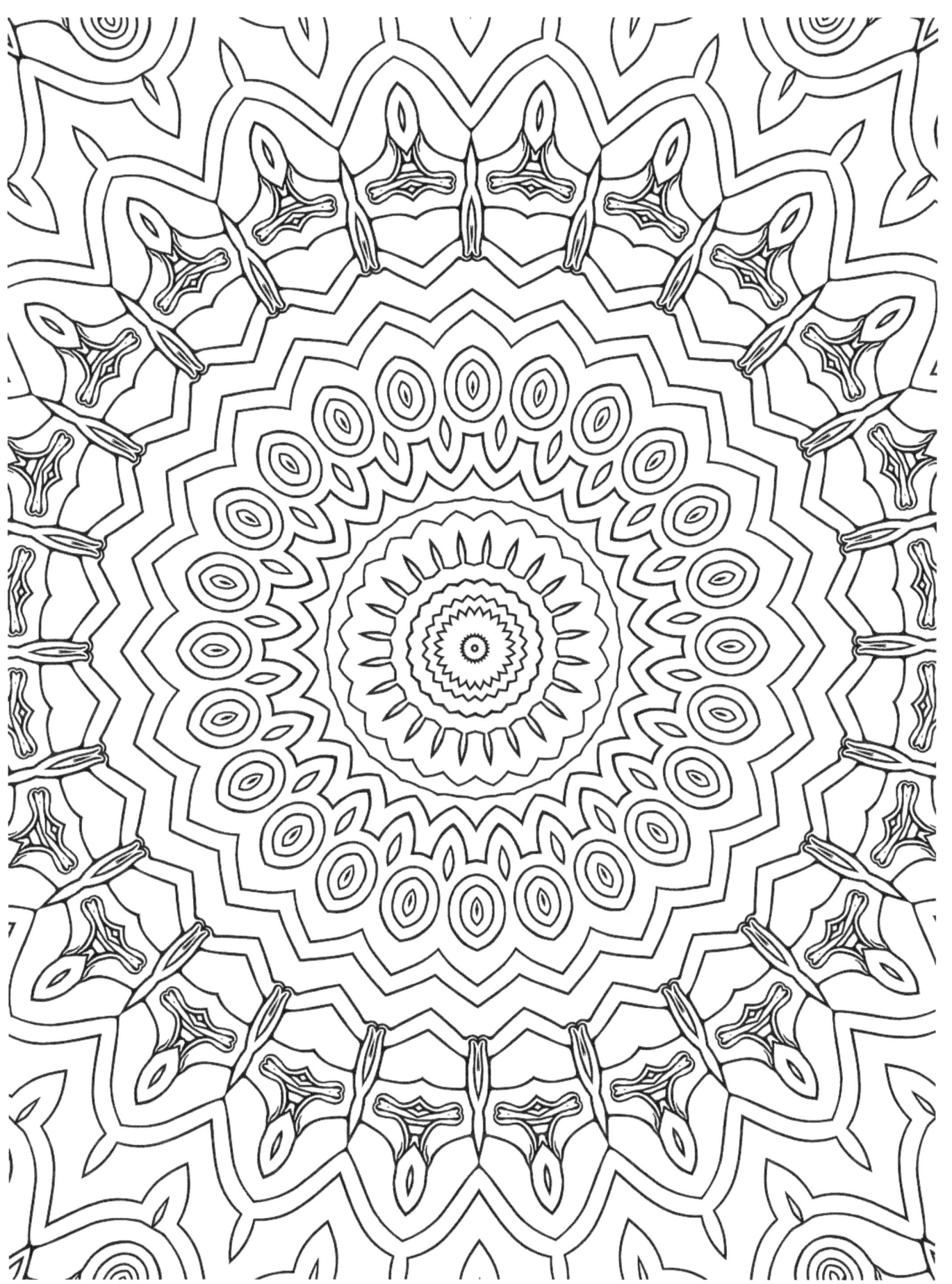

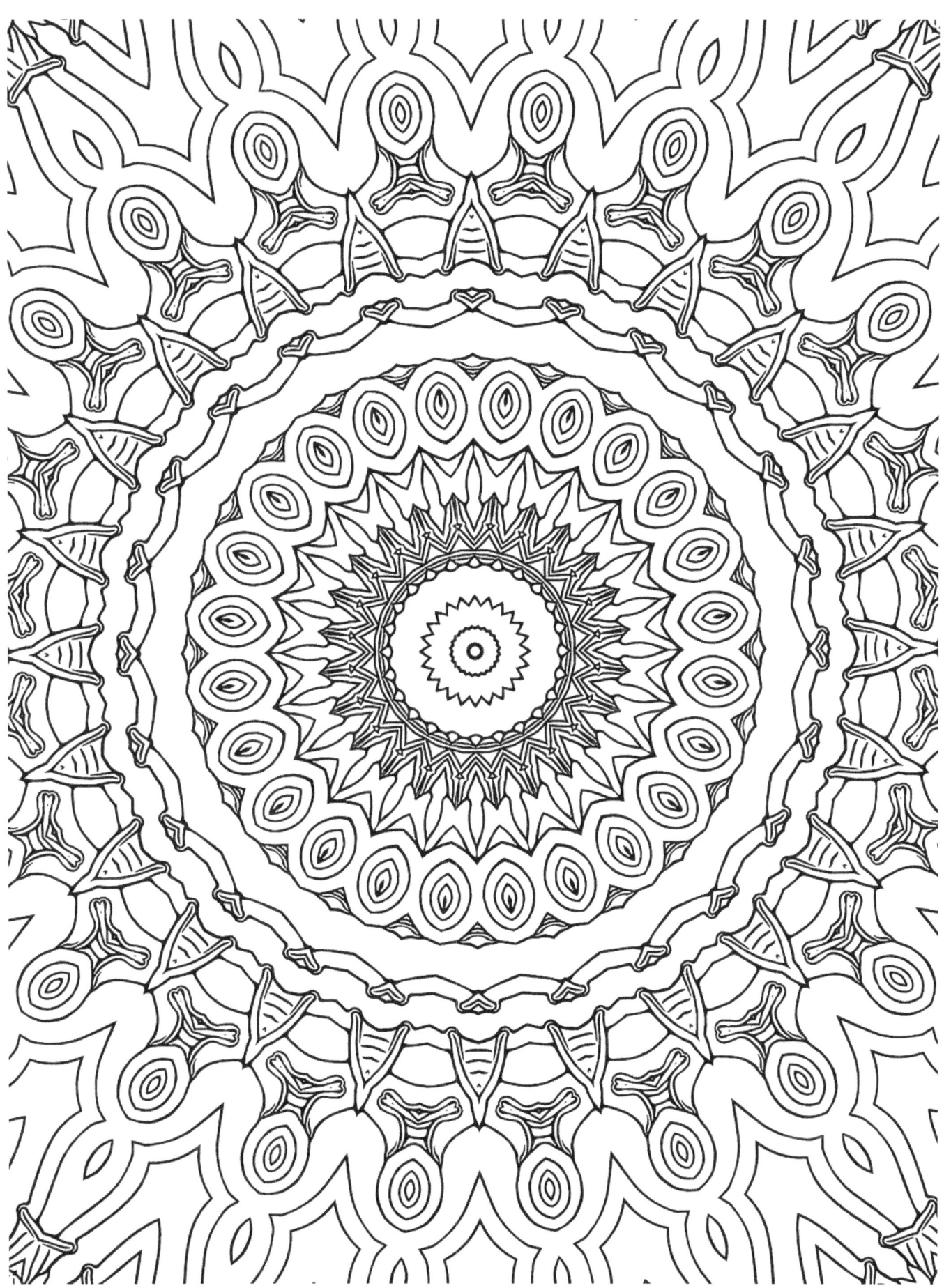

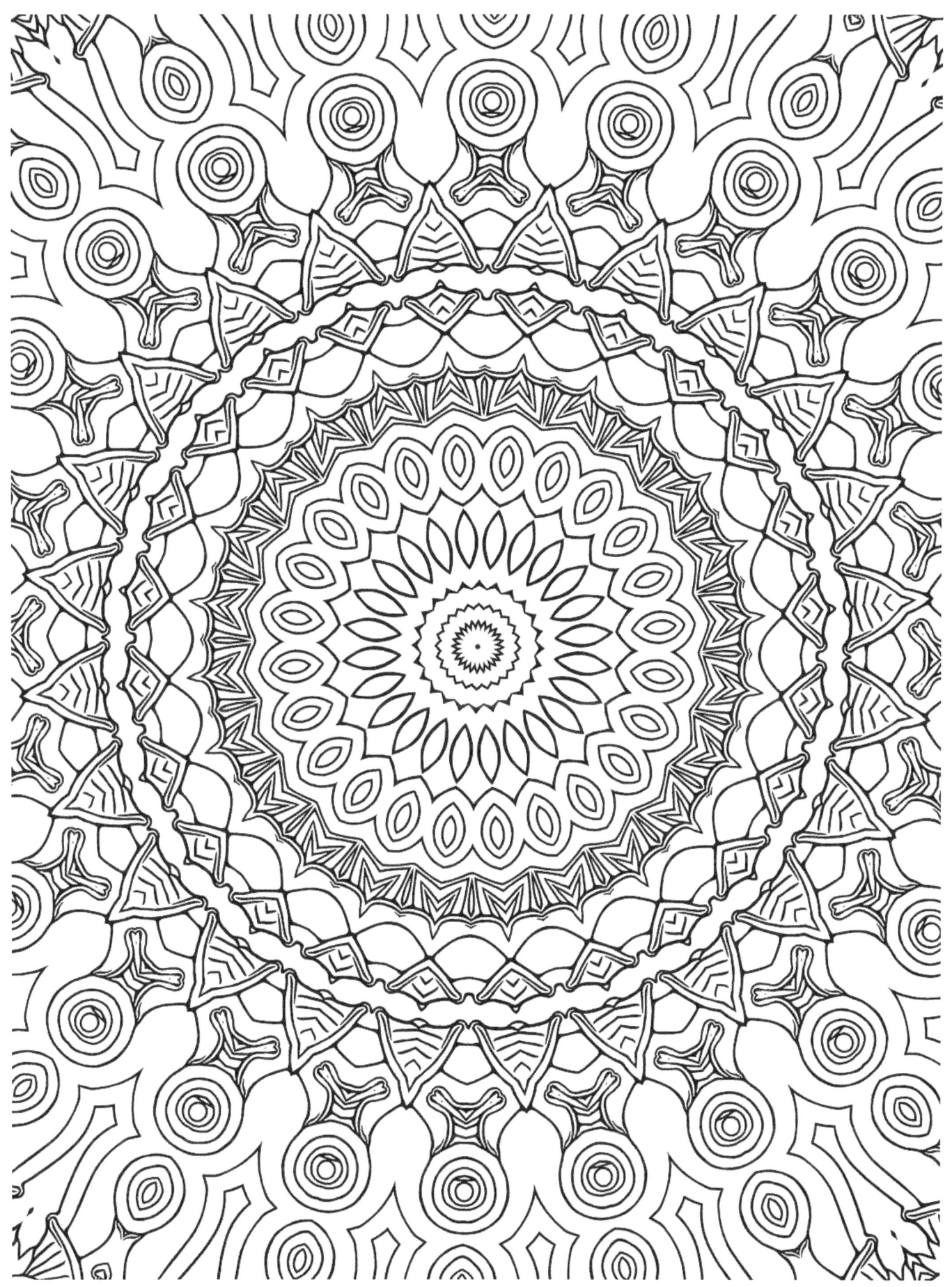

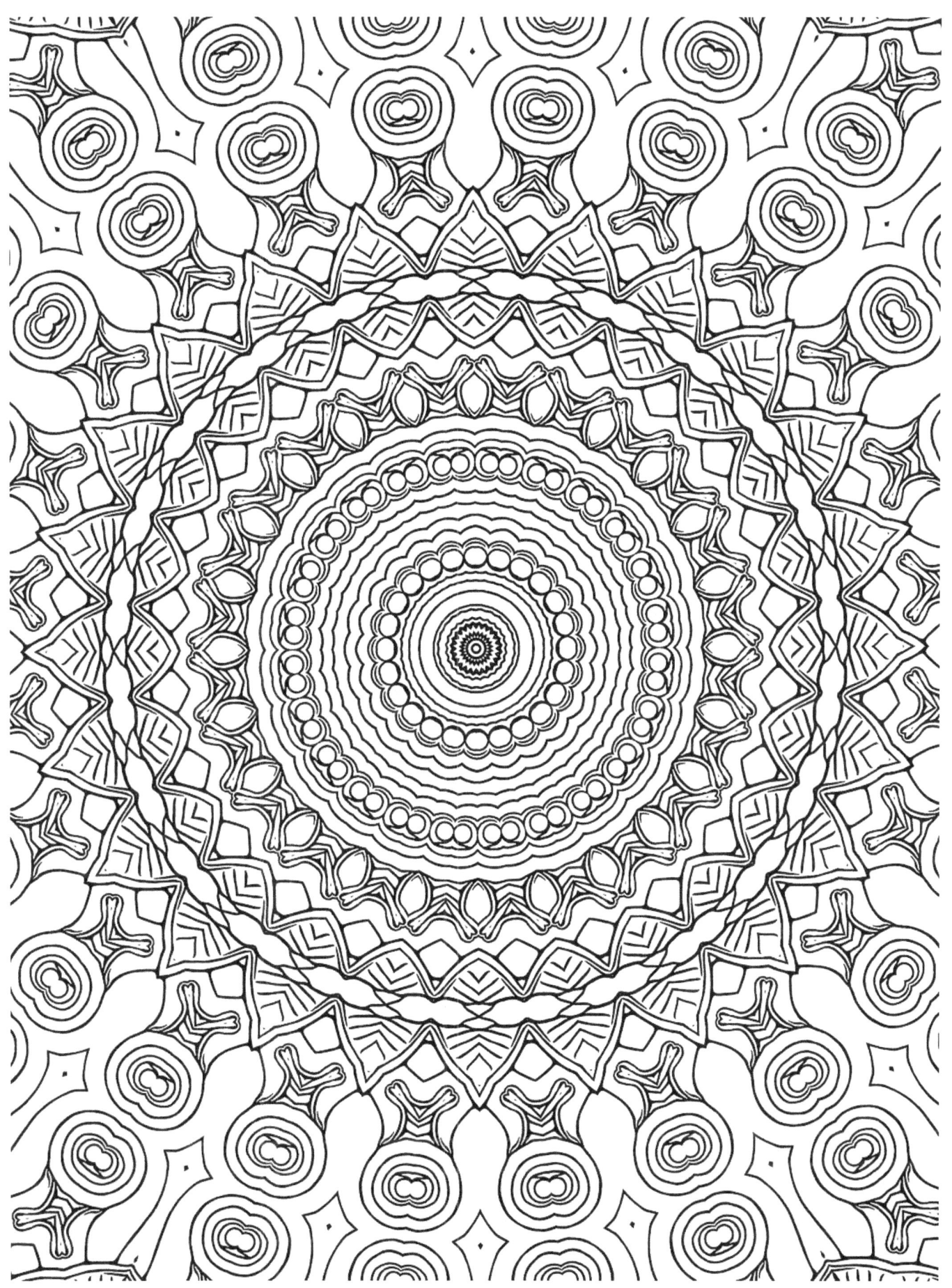

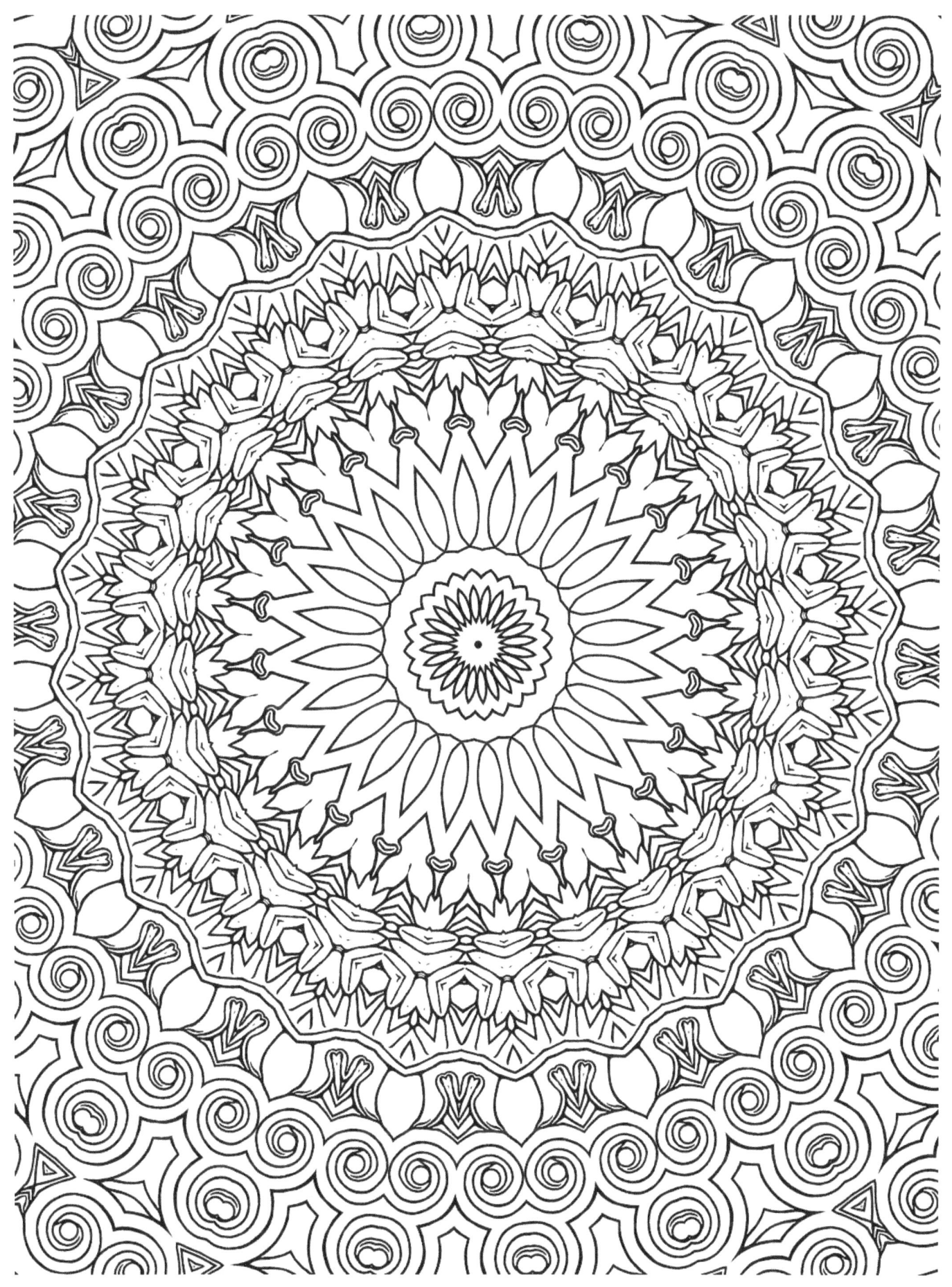

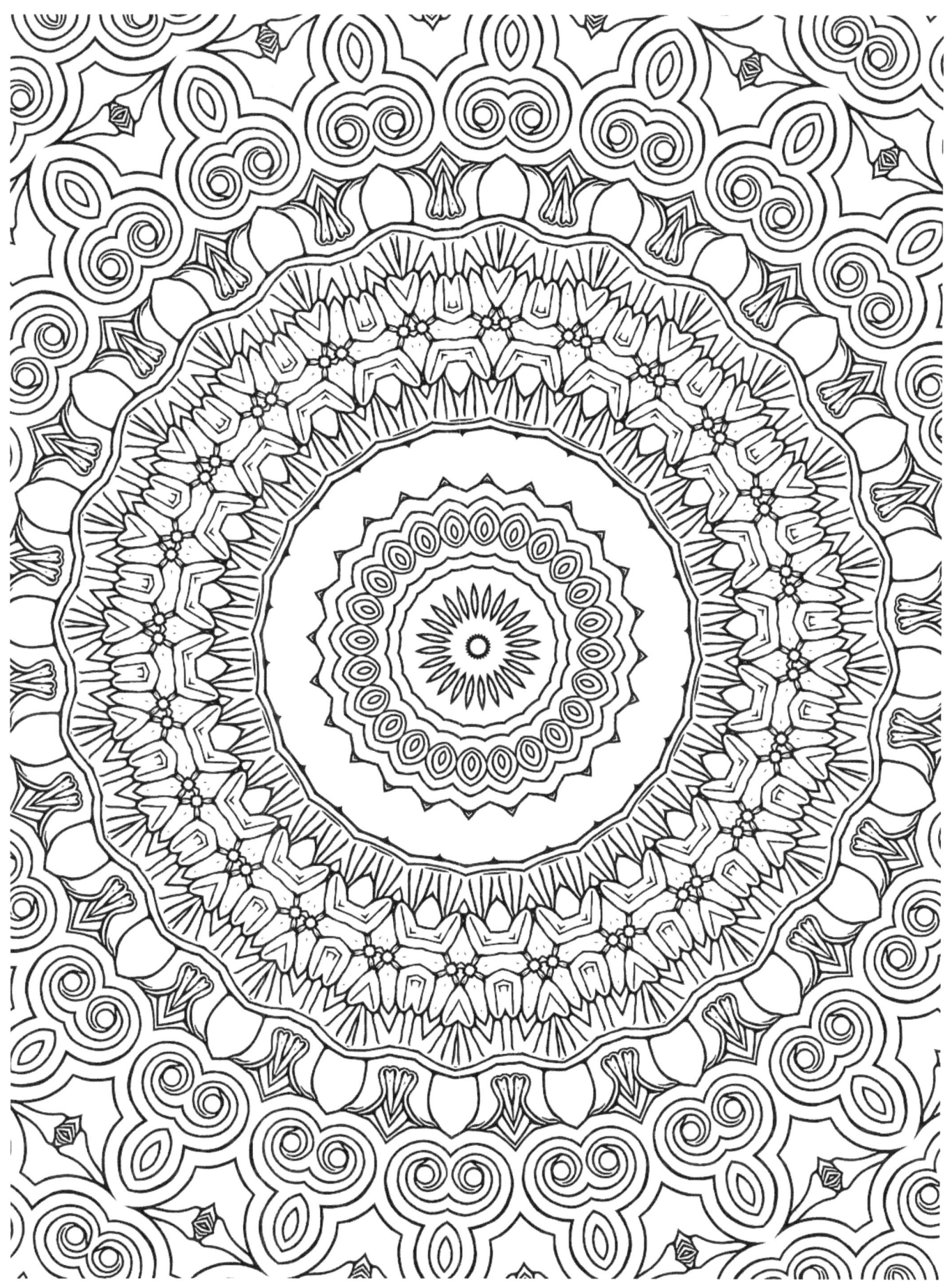